Indian Sculpture

TOWARDS THE REBIRTH OF AESTHETICS

Text and Sculpture

Carmel Berkson

ABHINAV PUBLICATIONS

abhinav publications

New Delhi

Cataloging in Publication Data–DK
Courtesy: D.K. Agencies (P) Ltd.<docinfo@dkagencies.com>

Berkson, Carmel, 1924-

Indian sculpture : towards the rebirth of aesthetics / text and sculpture, Carmel Berkson.
1. Sculpture, Indic. 2. Sculpture, Hindu. 3. Mythology, Hindu, in art. 4. Aesthetics, Indic.
I. Title.

DDC 730.954 22

First published in India 2009

Publishers
Shakti Malik
Abhinav Publications
E-37, Hauz Khas
New Delhi-110016 (INDIA)
Phones : 26566387, 26524658, 41655758
Fax : 91-11-6857009
E-mail : shakti@nde.vsnl.net.in
Website : http://www.abhinavexports.com

ISBN 81-7017-503-8

Printed at :
Archana
C-78, Okhla Industrial Area, Phase-I
New Delhi-110020

...artists, liberated from the burden of history, were free to make art in whatever way they wished, for any purposes they wished, or for no purpose at all. That is the mark of contemporary art and small wonder in contrast with modernism, there is no such thing as a contemporary art style.

...we might think about art after the end of art as if we were emerging from the era of art into something else, the exact shape and structure of which remains to be understood.

Arthur C. Danto,
After the End of Art and the Pale of History

Through the dark, cold and empty desolation
The wave cry, the wind cry, the vast waters
Of the petrel and the porpoise,
In the end is my beginning.

T.S. Eliot,
East Coker, Four Quartets

Books by Carmel Berkson

ELEPHANTA, THE CAVE OF SIVA (with Wendy Doniger and George Michell)

THE CAVES AT AURANGABAD

ELLORA, CONCEPT AND STYLE

THE LIFE OF FORM IN INDIAN SCULPTURE

THE DIVINE AND DEMONIAC

I wish to thank the Mitter Bedi Studio for technical services and Carmen Kagal for editorial comments.

Table of Contents

SECTION I

SECTION II

SECTION III

SECTION IV

SECTION I

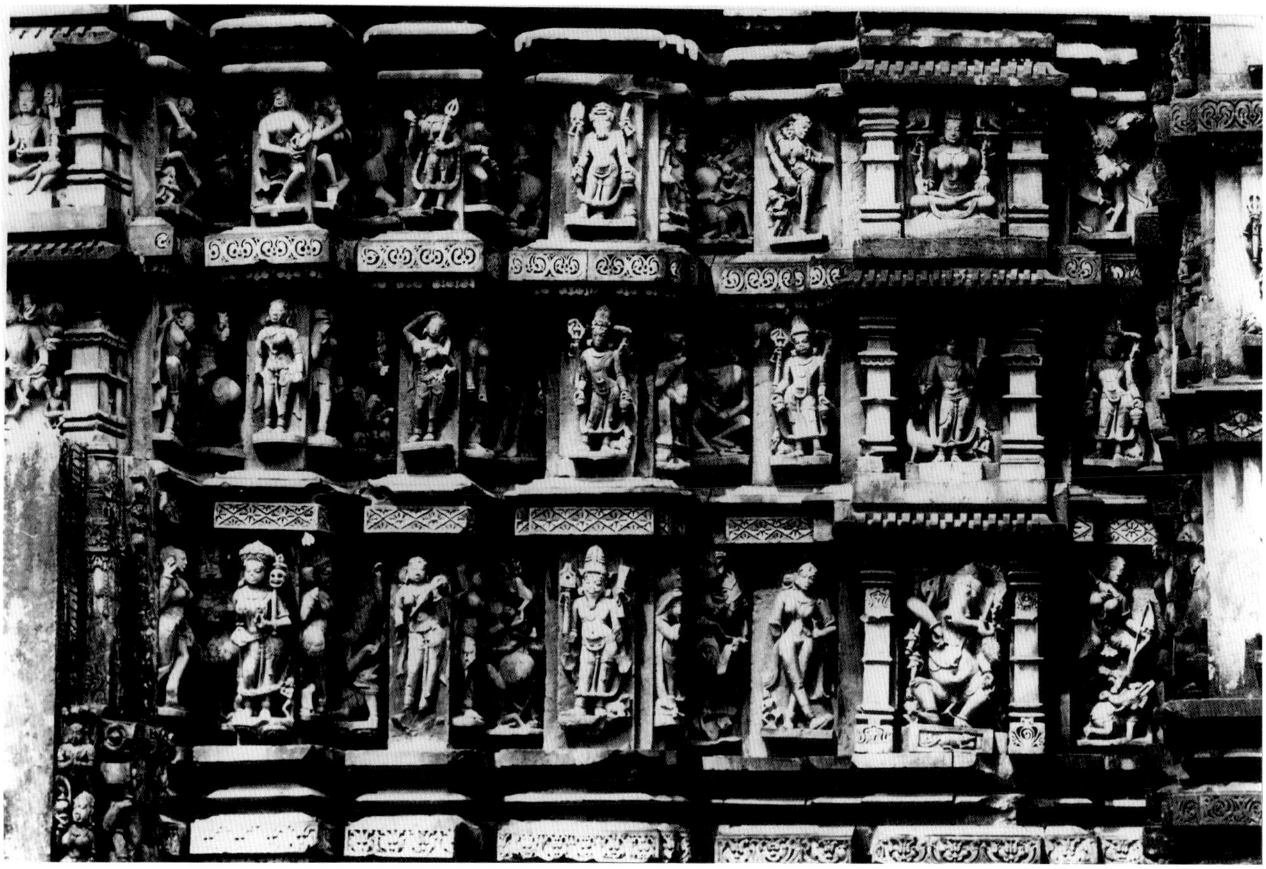

Fig. 1: **South Wall, partial view**

Markanda Temple
Maharashtra, early 11th c. C.E.

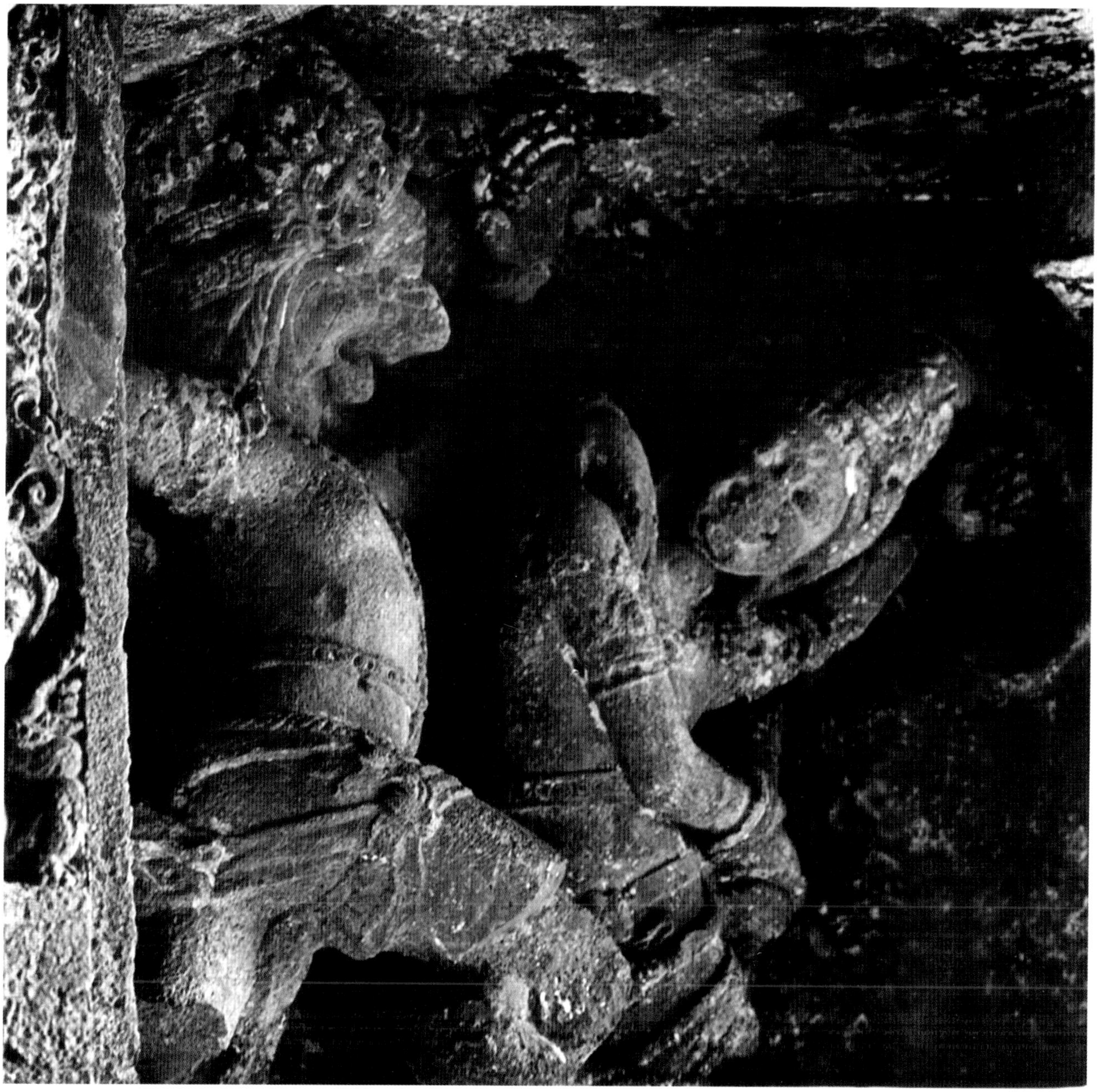

Fig. 2: **Statues are carved into deep mountain sanctuaries**

Narasimha/Hiranyakasipu,
Dasavatara, Cave 15, Ellora,
Maharashtra, 8th c. C.E.

Retrieving the Connection

I have been studying and photographing the sculpture of ancient India for many years. Consequently my primary intention in preparing this volume of images of my own statues is not merely to focus on exhibiting them. Rather I prefer to show that my work bears a definite, gratefully acknowledged connection with the magnificent sculpture of the past to which in structure, style and spirit I owe a great debt. This has led me to hope that others, especially young Indian sculptors, will find inspiration to begin the process of reawakening dormant, repressed cultural dynamics for the purpose of 'retrieving the connection'.

I hope I can join in the task of redirecting attention to what we can learn from the history of indigenous aesthetics and of the motivating philosophies, rituals and general ways of coping with life; and that with this revived understanding and focus, a connection with the form-life embedded in the cave temples and Hindu temples of India will have beneficial results for the aspiring artist. What is here is still very much a potent, forceful source of energy.

Statues are clustered on the walls of ancient Hindu temples; they are carved into deep mountain sanctuaries (Figs. 1, 2). Here is the dynamic life of form, evolving into complex mobile systems within which congruent convergencies and dissonant oppositions, in interminable interpenetrating processes, are in perpetual transformation. Many having been purloined, extracted from their original authentic locus, are to be found in the world's museums and in private collections.

Today, passion for the signifying icon is still one of the primary motivating forces in the civilization. As life support, local deities of varying names and every description are enshrined in urban, town, village, field, sacred precinct and highway abodes, providing succour to some hundred million devotees.

In the End is the Beginning: Time-Memory-Myth

The worshipper is in a state of longing for a connection with the mostly unconscious, intrinsic self (*atman*). One arrives in Ellora Caves in Maharashtra with repressions dominating, but very soon, in contact with nature and the sculpture and spaces in the cave, the restricting present time orientation fades. The state of mind of being outside of chronological, temporal time may last only for a short while, although adepts report a deeper involvement. All extraneous distractions are momentarily eliminated: birds, plants, sun, sky, colours, wind, statues, space seem not to be individuated. And then the worshipper has intimations of the meaning of the *linga* or the Buddha in the shrine. There is unity amongst ongoing, interactive processes within which the individual, now shorn of specificity and ego, seems to be involved. This is what in India is realized as intimations of Reality.

The average village person, even today, whose life has not been intruded upon by the industrial, technical and electronic transformations, lives in universal time – some of the temporal time. When that person approaches the image of a divinity, for example, standing in front of Siva as he dances, that dance is occurring in the present, but in all time as well, and when she pays homage, she 'feels peace', because then she is released from fragmentation of everyday consciousness. At 'heart' there is a sense of the Buddha's interrelationship of all phenomena, palpably felt. In India I have often observed that at this level, there are weaker, more porous boundaries between consciousness and the unconscious; between the idol and the worshipper there seems to be a stronger kinesthetic connection. The work of art becomes a reflection of the inner core of the perceiver.

The contents of all Indian sculpture represent that part of human consciousness where memory of time past merges with present awareness – with unbounded infinite imagery of previous human, even primordial experiences which are a-temporal and a-chronological. Past and present are combined in the image, as the timeless phantasmal realities of myths are embedded in the formal structures. The statues represent the composite of the symbols, ideas, and the cultural knowledge of the civilization – outside of concrete contemporaneity.

A point of departure for an inquiry into the symbolic world for Indians who have retained even a minimal connection with the mythological realities – and all do, of course – might be the sudden flash of memory of the ancient content of the myth, which now and again does spontaneously interrupt the daily fragmenting distractions all are subject to. Or the content of the myth may appear in dreams. At substratum levels, the transcendental and immediate worlds function simultaneously and are not in conflict. This experience may act as a directional signal to reactivate unconscious responses. As a stimulant for the perceptive person who has all his life been involved in symbols, the particular statue depicting a narrative is a mnemonic device, a remembrance, which can hold the past within it, with potential for activating cultural memory.

Art is not dead; it has a continuous existence in memory. Constant realities in human experience are embodied in art works in all eras. Energy is stored and will be contacted by new generations; it holds potential for renewal and return, for connection with eras of repeated cyclical transformations. The stored energy awaits release into new, but related, forms of expression. Though at this stage of art historical development, the experience of millennia of potency in art may momentarily be inhibited, repressed and sometimes even forgotten, when banality has run its course, the history of art will again be the foundational impetus for recovery and invention of new forms.

The cave temples are the storage houses of these contained energies, providing an opportunity for the contemporary sculptor to connect with the mindset of his forefathers for the purpose of recharging ancestral memories. These memories are bound eventually to be redirected into the mainstream of artistic will for the revitalization of spirit. Then hopefully there should be a rebirth of life force in Indian art. This accords with the Indian concept of time, during which there is a cyclical recurrence of universal processes. To paraphrase Eliot: in the end is the beginning.

Traditional Definition of Sculpture

In today's parlance in certain global corners, the terms 'sculpture', 'art' and 'interrelated material constructions' – subjects for polemic and dialogue – seem to be in transition; meanings are in question and are subject to various connotations and interpretations. It is therefore useful to indicate which were the accepted boundaries in India's past definitions and how they were transformed into the sculpture we now study on the extant monuments. These fundamental orientations are the essential definition of the topics in this study – how I use the terminology in this context as well. Hopefully it will become evident that those who believe in the continuity of art history and that art is by no means at end or dead, will agree to maintain the traditional meanings.

1. The statue has mass and palpable corporeality; it is a definite manifest presence, situated in a space surround, with which it is in interaction.

2. The statue is created out of natural materials with the use of hand-held tools. Perfect craftsmanship is prerequisite.

3. Underlying the formal material construct is an assumed grid oriented in vertical, horizontal, diagonal directions with a central point and circumference.

4. In different periods, the ritually standardized, prescriptive systems are varied in accordance with the orientations of the individual's internal promptings.

5. Except for the isolated figure or *linga* in the shrine (*garbha griha*), a single statue does not stand alone, but is an atomic unit in the interacting gestalt. In the matter of scale, the merest detail and the grandest size are made to be coordinate. Shapes are sculpted into complex configurations, with all units in active interrelation with all others. The cave panels are fields of forces – cauldrons of activity. The forces are either resolved or they remain in dynamic, continuous interplay.

Who is Doing Sculpture in India Today?

The exceptional talent for sculpture in India is evidenced, and always has been, by the teeming, protean creative outpourings over the centuries in all parts of the country. This skill is very much alive and well today in the various fields of sculpture. The cultural, economic, geographical and religious conglomerate that is India would naturally be responsible for diversity of expression, but the fundamental tendency to make imagery is in full force today. There definitely is no 'end of art' in sight!

I'd like to begin by relating an incident which occurred on one of my trips to the great temple site of Halebid in Karnataka. There I was approached by a young boy, probably not older than nine, whose family lived on the ground near the temple. It was obvious that they were rootless – in utter poverty. He asked me if I wanted to purchase a work of art. As is usual with boys in India, he was charming, and when I asked to see the work, he said he would make it then and there. Since I had already been on my way out I made an excuse, but he persisted and told me that within two hours, three would be ready, two for my friends in Bombay and one for myself. Then, true to his word, to my utter amazement, he presented me with three miniature stone sculptures of Hindu gods, meticulously carved, executed with skill and obviously with much care.

How many more of these unrecognized talented children are there all over the country? I can only have compassion for the loss of talent. Or maybe he is now grown and has managed to get himself connected with one of the following groups of sculptors. Hopefully!

1. 'Folk' art

Since probably eighty percent of Indians do not live in a technologically oriented mindset, sculptors are still actively creating all means of imagery for worship. If I were to scatter my own statues in various remote fields, I believe they would soon be co-opted as objects of worship. Village people will invest countless material objects with human, animal and natural forms, but primarily with such aura that is due to the deities they are connected with. These proliferations have no chronology; subjects do not arise from a particular priority but out of universal and age-old archetypes. Sometimes we can even detect all the threatening imagery of prehistory created by the descendants of an ancient hoary past.

It is difficult to specify or categorize the sculptors, who, all over the country, are still today producing an inexhaustible body of folk idols for village worship. In terms of numbers, unfortunately, many of the more talented have sought remunerative work which is market rather than worship oriented, and they no longer are in ignorance of what will sell. So in these cases the hand-to-material rhythms of work and the artist's prerogative to follow his own inner aesthetic compulsions have, in many cases, been abrogated.

Nevertheless, in every nook and cranny of India, in shrine or sacred precinct, on highways and in village shrines, for festivals and temple shrines, in all sizes (some enormous), shapes and individual interpretations, multitudinous imagery is still very much encountered. These are the village guardians or the chosen deity of the individual villager. They are made locally out of any and all materials, carved in stone, wood or modelled in man-made materials.

What *can* be observed with certainty is that there is no absolutely fixed distinction between folk and the 'higher' art – which had been created during those particular periods when patrons, artists and rulers formed an interactive system reaching heights of aesthetic greatness. There is only a linear continuum involved in a vast interacting assemblage of diverse imagery arising out of a multiplicity of conceptions and interpretations of each individual's personal perceptions. The range is from the merest single shaped stone, via imagery emerging entirely from the untrained mind of a talented person, who, like a child today, expresses innately originated conceptions and patterning processes. Each artist will conceive of reality according to his own inner visions.

There will also be imagery either negligibly or more seriously influenced by what the sculptor has observed in his mental and physical vicinity, depending of course on the many factors of his particular experience. If he has been in contact with the great temples, with a keen eye for form and sculptural relationships on their walls, traces will naturally enter his own work. Others will base their statues on textually constructed models, although each will vary as to what degree they approximate the generally accepted prescribed fundamentals.

We are swimming in a vast sea of immense variations from all periods and all parts of the country. This can never be rigidly classified as 'folk'. Preferably we might simply consider each image on its own merits and enjoy the protean world of living forms. Ultimately all these outpourings reference a common, indefinable Enormity, beyond the specificity of the particular image.

2. Contemporary imagery

The great majority of sculptors today are occupied in creating sculpture for public display. In the cities and towns all over India, large bronze images of Gandhi,

Shivaji on a horse, Ambedkar and a host of minor political leaders are cast in foundries, displayed outdoors for political edification and styled according to neo-classic, nineteenth century, British influences.

Then for festivals there are the large *pandals* (floats) of Durga in Kolkata and environs and statues of Ganapati in Maharashtra – large painted plaster and clay imagery for eventual immersion. And all over the country the sculptor is called upon to portray colourful large imagery to enliven many diverse occasions. Styles range from copies of models to myriads of spontaneous individual expressions.

3. The traditional sculptor

The traditional sculptor has been trained by his family or by a famous *sthapathi*, or today, at government schools. *Sastric* (traditional textual) rules concern iconographically predetermined statues of divinities and their retinues; familiar age-old hand tools for carving stone and wood and modelling clay and wax for transformation into bronze are used. While output varies in quality, in the final analysis, there has been little or no transformation in the fundamental Hindu, Buddhist and Jain themes depicted. Statues are sold either for worship in temples or in home shrines, or they are for sale at government and private outlet stores.

An entirely unique carver, Sudarshan Sahoo, of Puri, isn't himself descended from a traditional family, but is blessed with great natural talent, so much so that his imagery – in skill, spirit and reliance on ancient rules and materials – causes one to fantasize that he is an *avatara* of the great genius designers of the medieval temples. He is a man of many perspectives and can also carve stone in any number of different styles; he has produced hundreds of variations on the standard themes, always keeping to the traditional narrative and producing authentic works of art. His school trains sculptors whose apprenticeship often lasts up to ten years or more.

A few private companies support specific artists who still work in traditional styles. In the South today, many artists, most from traditional sculptors' families, will not veer from the strict rules, and so their complex statues bear great resemblance to those of the ancient schools, such as of the Chola or Vijayanagar dynasties. Occasionally individuals do exhibit these works in urban galleries, but today there isn't much interest.

In other cases, however, while statues do rely heavily on ancient compositions, on modular specification from *silpa sastras* and on a grand variety of traditional subjects, there are those sculptors who deviate from the great medieval prototypes, some slightly and others now more radically. Or, as is becoming more common, they make statues with variations on traditional themes, allowing themselves flights of imagination and a personal style, at times with the result that while the carving skills are very much still intact, the product is a more modernized, often standardized, perhaps less authentic work.

4. Modern art school educated sculptors

They have often been trained in colonial styles. The father of Om Prakash Shirgaonkar, who cast my statues, learned the craft from the British at J.J. School of Art in Bombay. Today students are familiar with the history of western art and are much influenced by it. Although they have been to the Indian sites, they have not concentrated exclusively on Indian temple and cave temple sculpture or on the bronze tradition; their memory of, and connection with, the magnificent heritage is weak.

As they fashion their individual statues, some students do incorporate indigenous subject matter into their work; but the underlying structure, the style and other techniques of the past have been abandoned. Very few students today realize that the great sculptures of the past are a wonderful source and inspiration and hold within great hints about how new styles can evolve, based on lessons from the past. This is my primary concern. Unfortunately, often the tendency is to make efforts to stay within the fashionable, by now more familiar western oriented Post Modern movements, especially as many are sought after by the proliferating, mostly commercially oriented galleries (see pages 18-20). But I'm happy to say that this does not apply to those very sensitive and serious artists who are in touch with their roots and intend to tell the world about their convictions!

5. Self-trained sculptors

Some sculptors, in various parts of the country, have not been to art school, but their natural talent and the primal need to externalize their visual, emotional and life experiences have dictated their artistic choices. Most artists in this category have had very little contact with contemporary western movements. Their work is entirely eclectic, a hodge-podge of styles, all very little influenced by television, media and advertising. A plethora of bulls and buffaloes, mother and child, farmers and animals, the pulchritude of village ladies and, of course, the gods and goddesses of India and many other more or less realistic references to the daily life of the average person, has populated the galleries with Indian subjects close to the heart of the average Indian visitor. People seem to enjoy connecting to familiar subjects.

Winds from the West

If, by the exhibits in the Indian urban circuits, one were to judge the extent to which sculptors have been enticed into Post Modern movements, it might be assumed that a huge influx of western ideas and influences have penetrated their minds. In effect, as we have observed, the general population of Indian sculptors do operate in various other spheres. Only the economically and educationally privileged sculptors and their coteries, with ever watchful eye towards the benefits of the global art scene, have been more seriously oriented in the direction of international trends than towards the sculpture of India's millennial past. This magnificent past is well documented, and every school child has been exposed to the abundance of sculptural forms. It is thus interesting to reflect upon some of the perceptual and cognitive deviations evident in so many contemporary works. A climate of disorientation has caused unease, and there have been repercussions. It seems appropriate to consider the resultant effects of the transformed western ideologies on Indian sculptors and on those in control of the art culture industry – the gallery/media/critic nexus.

In India, post colonial veneer had provided the impetus for a predilection towards the west, even though Post Modernism has exclusively developed out of the twentieth century western historical experience. That some sculptors' orientations have shifted from indigenous influences must be admitted. The general trend has been to wrench art and artist out from the historical cultural context – the involvement within religio-mythological beliefs and traditional aesthetic values. In danger of becoming a mere unit in a technological and market controlled infrastructure, to be commodified as makers of saleable products, urban sculptors may actually now be in crisis.

In the west, as a result of the general malaise of spirit at mid-twentieth century, after the horrors of two devastating world wars, many young artists abandoned previously accepted agendas, including belief in god, hope for positive societal changes and purposeful movements in history. History itself was jettisoned, as being too much of a nightmare to justify its preservation! They questioned every foundational accepted concept; they lost faith in the predominant values of their predecessors and of western societies. Most important of these values were in the realm of humanism, ethics, cultural conventions and many of the institutional bulwarks of society in general. Even Modern art, with its emphasis on transcendental aspirations and pure abstract form, was dismissed as anachronistic.

It was a spiritual impoverishment influencing a narrow response by a post-war generation of young rebels who had watched new wars on television. As they emerged from childhood, they were jolted out of humanistic expectations and illusions. What more advantageous response to the shock of waking to the realities of history than to deny its very existence? The baby of traditional art was summarily discarded with the waters of the awakening. The rebellion was primarily focused against the values in art of the 'bourgeois' society, although ironically most had grown up in this very milieu and had reaped its benefits. Needless to add that it is the derided middle class that have now staked their claim on Post Modernism and its successor movements, or its non-movements.

In the meantime, post-World War II western society was being transformed; sculptors felt impelled to begin investigation into and expression of new revelations about what it was like to live in a world threatened by nuclear war and increasingly complex industrial, technological, then electro-chemical discoveries, so much of which was under corporate control and was being defined as 'progress'. They contemplated their role in society and made attempts to come to grips with all that was new.

Under this influence, in the process of sidetracking and dismissing the artistic glories of the past, many urban western oriented sculptors in India seem to have lost their major links with the underlying spiritual content of indigenous sculpture. Negation and deconstruction alone, however, obviously never could be sustained as a cultural paradigm for long, as no civilization has ever before been able to survive psychically without creating symbols for the purpose of confrontation with temporal and spiritual realities. Thus turning inward, they took courage in narcissistic pride and negation of romantic illusions or any illusions.

Disillusioned, and like their western counterparts, they became associated with what seemed to be the constancies in physical laws and scientific a-moral truths, and these sometimes became the substitute for their discarded religious and traditional values. Some of these sculptors adopt artistic sensibilities to the contemporary scientific world view, where they feel at home and comfortable. Technically inspired work, dubbed as 'sculpture', concerns what is believed to be scientific reality. They no longer copy nature, but study its processes, and they assert that out of scientific investigations and conclusions, new forms will emerge. There seems to be a hope that, if their sculpture is a living model of quantum reality, if much attention is directed to subatomic conditions and to the study of scientific models, a more intuitive understanding of the realities of life would thereby become known to them.

It might be possible therefore to find some common ground between contemporary scientific views and the ancient theoretical and artistic assumptions, to consider whether or not, in point of fact, the ancient world had not already examined a body of thought that is under scientific investigation today. If this is proven to be true, we might then be able to suggest certain avenues by means of which Indian sculptors can be spiritually and psychologically renewed by reconnecting with their own past.

It would seem that the primary issue for a contemporary young Indian sculptor is to consider how she is situated at a particular position along the continuum of traditional/contemporary/global transformations. It is not a question of fusion, but an effort to re-examine periods in her history which have focused on how the individual relates to the grand totality. There is too much danger that the onrush and intrusive multitude of disparate currents coming at her in tornado force might very well result in the fragmentation of her own self identity. Our task might be seen to be a search for a common root ground between atrophied, too sternly imposed rules of the past with a more permissive modern vision, without the loss of what are the essential qualities of an authentic art form – based on the two thousand year experience in India – so as not to lose touch with what is a veritable encyclopedia of knowledge concerning the making of great sculpture.

Current Concerns

I have been suggesting all along that there are enormous opportunities for alienated Indian sculptors to make an effort to become re-involved at serious levels with the renowned works of sculpture which await them at the major sites. Re-entrance and confrontation is most likely to ignite repressed responses. When a genuine connection with the indigenous past is initiated – really never can it be severed – deeper insights may be aroused.

Taking for granted that a universal need for the aesthetic experience is an elemental imperative, the ultimate goal of world art should be defined as the coordination of transcendental and sensible responses. The encounter with the work of art as experienced today by those who worship images is to be distinguished from a genuine aesthetic interplay of responses only partially. The average Indian worshipper, who invests the idol with divine attributes and the modern urban secular art lover, who arrives at the gallery or museum, will share the expectation of entering into a sacred area and will prepare for an extraordinary experience. What for the first is a sense of transcendent awe, will stimulate for the latter, if the displayed artwork is of authentic quality, a genuine aesthetic shock.

Even while the technological society creates a shift in values in regard to the work of art – from cultic to display – aura need not be lost today; it depends entirely on the artist who, in a democracy, is free to respond to his own promptings. Aura is not merely a product of ritual or the impositions of a religious or traditional society. It emerges from within individual and cultural consciousness. There is no need for the artist to be in service to the market.

The true artist lives in his inner world; it is here, in fact, that aura is generated. Historically, never have patrons or priests controlled either the responses of the genius artist or the genuinely inner-oriented worshipper whose *atman* is not subject to outside dictation. Once external factors come into play, art always suffers the intrusion. I hope that the youth of this country will take advantage of the opportunity that I have had to be in contact with the enormously rich heritage, with some of the greatest sculptors the world has ever encountered. They have left a tremendous legacy – forms which will always be available for reinterpretations and integration, forms emerging from the very heart of the psyche of each individual. It is here that common human needs for an aesthetic experience can be wonderfully satisfied.

In a technologically oriented society, it would seem that the true sculptor will eventually be forced to pay attention to universal and permanent processes of consciousness. If she is disturbed and understands that society has the capacity to threaten the individual's central core – the connection with private, internally generated responses, the *atman*, and if she believes that resistance to the onslaught is possible, she may perhaps find a way to combat the emptiness and barrenness which might very well be the result of being involved with concerns other than aesthetics.

With the support of her indigenous millennial beliefs about reality and the processes of creation, that person will come to know how to externalize the innermost essence, the internal emotions, beliefs and emblems of herself, and even though she might then not be in synchrony with the latest marketable expressions of her particular community, the true artist will be so busy reflecting on the general human condition with which she herself *is* in synchrony, that she will bear the rejections – hopefully with appreciation of the irony of the situation – with humour and acceptance of the realities of the divine *lilas*.

Ancient insights/contemporary concerns

It is, nevertheless, not difficult for me to empathize with those sculptors who, in art schools and through art journals, have been exposed to the contemporary negations of art and history very much still operating in galleries from New York to Singapore. A new breed of urban Indian artist is part loyal son or daughter, held fast to a relatively closed family organization and part separated individual artist, involved in the ongoing art scene. I am told that what I see as an intrusion of western influence, for these people is merely an overlay, and their true self is still genuinely a loyal Indian son or daughter. But perhaps they may very well see their new role in the western negation of traditional art as an analogy with their own rescue from a psychologically disturbing situation. That of course will be known only to the individual.

A good way to initiate a dialogue with Indian sculptors who are concerned with issues and challenges that face them today, is to isolate features each shares with her ancestors. It is important to recognize, as we have seen, that there are seminal analogies between the new science and the intuitions of the ancient sages, artists and architects. The connections between eastern philosophies and modern quantum physics may thus be the precise point of possible interaction. The recognition of this might provide the sought-after pathway for an approach which has the potential for coordinating ancient Indian wisdom with contemporary scientific discoveries.

This seems to be a positive approach. It allows the artist to clear the air sufficiently so that she can make the attempt to separate that which is destructive to her independence and individuality and that which will enhance and presumably give rise to new and vital insights. That it is imperative to disregard superstitions, fundamentalist rigidity in regard to caste and hoary practices has become obvious to all. On the other hand, if she is inclined to dig deeply into traditional Indian thought processes, she will find that there are important analogies with the post-Newtonian, twentyfirst century restructuring of conceptions of reality. If the dichotomy between the existing popular culture and the wisdom inherent in the perennial religions (as manifested in the art of sculpture and temple architecture) can be brought into direct focus, a new beginning is likely to emerge. As the incrustations of the past are removed, *darshan* made at the monuments will illuminate the elemental concepts there and can be studied along with those that are under investigations in regard to the physical world today. Although traditional Indian concepts have not been proven by means of modern experimental analytic methods, the proof is in the physical structures and the vast resource of oral and written texts. To those in India who sculpted, danced, made music and wrote poetry during the past millennia certain contemporary scientific ideas would very well have sounded familiar:

The Buddha speaks of interconnection of all phenomena, the never independent aggregates and of a universe that is not subject to separation or differentiation. Scientists speak of pattern, structure, system, patterns of organization common to all systems, communities of organisms, emergence of order, complex networks of interacting phenomena, patterns of circular causality. Perhaps, on a professional level, young physicists here in India might be willing to elaborate on these conceptions, to define the intricacies. Or perhaps in order to begin the process, sculptors might work at the sites with the physicists to combine intuitive, scholarly and scientific approaches.

Most of the ideas are applicable to all periods of the history of Indian sculpture, even though styles change. Ellora can be mentioned as one site where it has become obvious that the intuitive wisdom responsible for this particular universe/system can be approached as an example to be studied in concordance with contemporary scientific orientations.

One can approach the thirty-four caves either with regard to the minutest detail or as multiple, unified systems in a grand totality, consisting of systems within systems within systems, applying the scientific terminology which turns out to be helpful when it comes to verbalizing what is there. The emphasis too is on the continuum of metamorphosing interdependent phenomena. There is *guna* interaction, emergence, evolution, entropy; there is order and fluctuation in order, transfer of energies, single forms as units in complexity, imaging biological processes, and certainly, all phenomena are connected and dynamically integrated. And more. A perceptive spectator who studies the cave phantasmagoria carefully will eventually be able to observe the site as a paradigm for some of the pre-eminent modern concepts.

SECTION II

Mental Events

Recently neural science has greatly advanced our knowledge of brain structure and of the dynamic interplay of non-linear neural connections and working networks of perpetually shifting configurations. It is not yet possible to differentiate accurately the exact nature of the relationship between the physical brain and human consciousness, which is considered to be a function distinct from its physical source, while simultaneously it is dependent on it. But it has become apparent that the externalizations of pattern and structure imagery on to matter are the projections of innate, immanent biological and cognitive processes generated in the human brain/mind, while consciousness provides awareness of life forces. Animals with or without 'mind' also instinctively create complex structures with underlying patterns. All around us nature teaches about pattern, structure and system.

In India we have evidence of organizational processes in the shapes of the bricks of the Vedic altar and of the altar itself as proof of a complex mathematical system. The altar signified the centre of the universe out of which Agni emanated as energy. Pattern underlies the foundational plan of the *vastupurusamandala*, a square diagram with central point for construction of Hindu temples. Throughout millennia, and all over India *chakra, mandala, yantra*, in daily ritual use, all point to an organizational imperative operative as generic patterning processes.

Contemporary concepts regarding the immanent structure of grammar in language have been found to be applicable to other disciplines. In diverse cultures, pattern, structure and systems have always been essential to the definition of sculpture. In India the *silpa sastras* codify patterning and modular instructions for sculptors. We have evidence from myriad examples that all of traditional sculpture had as its generating stimulus the structuring mechanism of the human brain.

So from which precise area of the brain/mind did the traditional sculptor's deep rooted instinct for patterning come, or whether he had a fixed image of this pattern prior to the initiation of his creation, or even whether it emerged from his unconscious during the process, cannot be precisely known at this stage of neural investigations. However, the artist did always have an intimation of pattern, and it became a necessary, primal element in the organization of his conceptions and a fundamental source of the unity of the work.

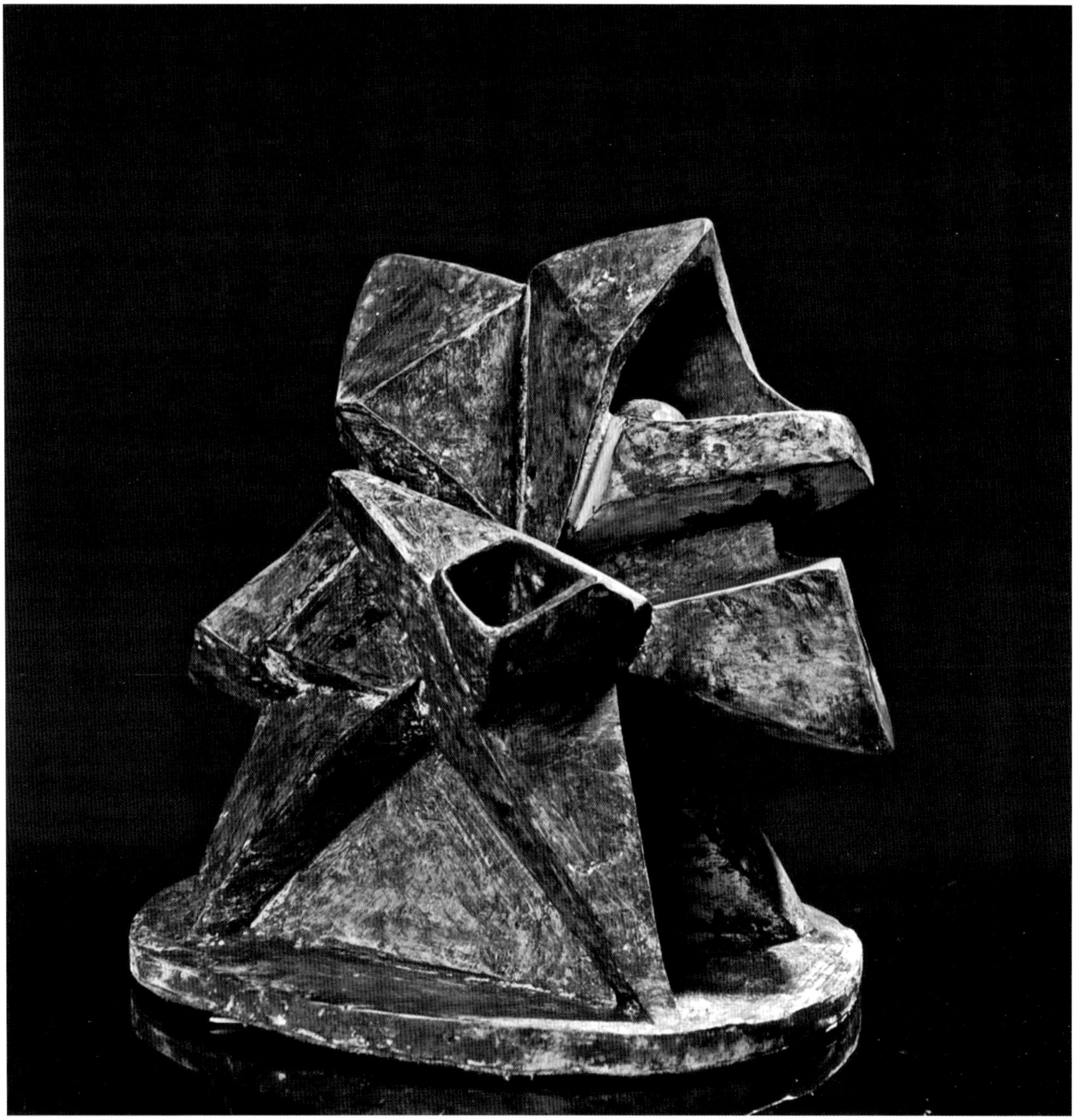

Fig. 3: **Centrifugal and centripetal oscillations between *bindu* and circumference**

Abstract Forms
Carmel Berkson,
Bronze, 12" x 8" x 10"

Pattern (*Panjara*)

We owe the Swiss artist/scholar, Alice Boner and her associate, Pandit Sadasiva Rath Sharma, a debt of gratitude for publishing the secret and rare manuals recorded by master sculptors and architects in medieval times; they concern the application by the sculptor of the diagrammatic pattern (*panjara*) on to the stone prior to initiating the work. Before these were recorded as written texts, however, the *panjara* was no doubt originally intuited by the sculptors, as for many previous centuries they had been involved in the actual experience of carving sculpture in rock. As they worked the pattern emerged automatically.

Pattern is a prime constituent of human thought (Fig. 3); art is a language which encodes inherent brain structuring potential. The *panjara* has its roots in biological oscillations of neural activity in the human brain. In a coordinating process between brain and mind, a visual image of pattern becomes available to consciousness. In all precedent periods of art history, in all cultures, and throughout the many centuries of India's sculptural productions, sculptors were impelled to project a latent patterning potential and to fix it in organic matter.

Most traditional Indian sculpture, but not all, whether created for shrine, temple wall or cave temple panel, has either a two-dimensional or an orthogonal *panjara* as its foundation. The *panjara* is a *yantric* grid, with central point (*bindu*), horizontal, vertical and diagonal vectors and a circumference. The sculptor draws this diagram on to the surface of the work and then carves shapes to accord with the underlying pattern. Then the constant centrifugal and centripetal oscillations, back and forth between *bindu* and circumference and along the vertical and horizontal and diagonal vector lines, become apparent. Potential for circularity is a product of brain functioning as well and is involved in the structure of the finished work.

The *panjara* is the fundamental root source of traditional sculpture, the projection of the latent potential for patterning in the mind of the sculptor. It is here that structure is initiated. While relying on traditional precepts, texts and practices, in his creative frenzy, the ancient sculptor was simultaneously aware of the automatically emerging pattern. It provides the underlying, non-material stability for the dynamic interplay of form relationships, fixing proportion, measure, order out of chaos. It is the mechanistic underpinning for the interactions of structural elements with content and internally generated energies, and it is responsible for the coherent structure of the finished statues. Vectors of the *panjara* interact and create a sense of energetic mobility.

During the process of modelling or carving, the structure is intuited, while the pattern having been erased by the supervening forms remains, but it is not visible. Still, the ordering process of the *panjara*, the immanent presence, will be available to an aware spectator whose own brain processes are in contact with those of the ancient sculptor.

Structure

While structure has a separate existence and is without substance, it nevertheless is inseparable from the life of forms. Structure is the coordination of perpetually mobile, interacting elements; here it refers to the deep, non-linear, immanent but non-material organization of basic shapes in the statue or configuration of statues in the cave temple panels. The structure is inherent in the particular relationships to one another of visible complex, multi-layered integrated animated forms with others in the individual statues and with the framed panels, the parts of which are mutually interdependent and are in constant flux within these related, energized fields.

Interaction of volumes with space in the fields will produce a sense of movement, rhythm, dynamic contrasts, balanced and distorted thrusts, torsion, ambiguity, content and many other implicated features. In Indian sculpture (and in my own), structure does not imply closure; outward force with indefinite extension is implied.

Pattern underlies structure and is implicit in structure. While the *panjara's* lines and orthogonal armature are fixed and immobile, in the structure, parts are not stabilized but are perennially in transformation and flux within a system. The horizontal, vertical, diagonal and circular indications of the *panjara* are functioning in the mobile structure. Because it is only implicit, structure is not available for optical observation, so its presence will have to be intuited.

It is interesting to find out in which way the student and visitor to the caves will be able to access the structure in order to gain a deeper appreciation of the artwork in all its complexities. With a concentrated effort and elimination of all extraneous stimuli, the process of visual confrontation will activate what at first seems to be a static situation. Even while the elements are physically stabilized, the image is instantaneously transferred via the eye, to the brain; neural processes are activated to form the mental image which is the structure; then the inherent organization of the panel becomes apparent in consciousness. This will happen automatically only after serious studies are made. Forms will then appear to be in a mobile configuration, observed as a gestalt, or whole, within which there is mobility and interaction of parts. Shapes will fall into place.

Style differences are the integration of forms on to different underlying *panjaras*. For example, in Cave 21, Ellora, in *Siva Dancing in Lalita* (Fig. 4), the 'classic' style

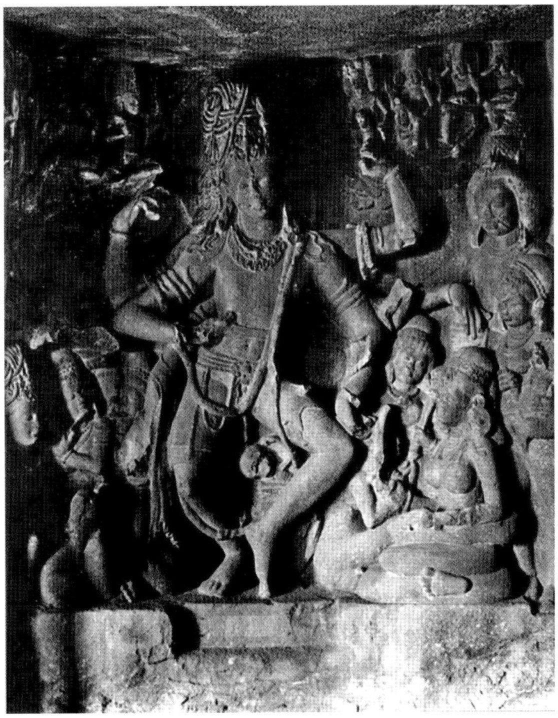

Fig. 4: **The 'classic' style will show the verticality as predominant** Siva Dancing in Lalita, Ramesvara, Cave 21, Ellora, Maharashtra, 6th c. C.E.

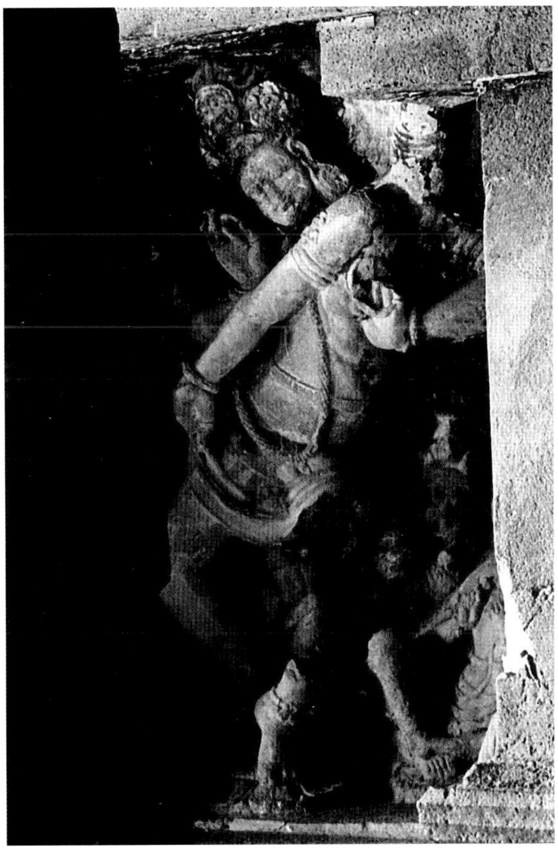

Fig. 5: **Diagonal vectors are emphasized** Siva Dancing in Lalita, Dasavatara, Cave 15, Ellora, Maharashtra, 8th c. C.E.

will show the verticality as predominant, while in Cave 15 (Fig. 5) and Cave 16, diagonal vectors are emphasized.

How the spectator accesses the structure that was in the mind of the artist

There is an analogy between the creative will of the artist and the biological processes of nature. The artist and the perceptive spectator share the immanent physical laws which operate within the brain/mind of each. The sculptor was impelled to invest the statue or panel with a reflection of his own mental processes, to encode structure. Should he shed his outward defences and put himself into a contemplative mood, the visitor to the caves will prepare himself for an aesthetic experience. There is pleasure and shock during the confrontation, which is the result of the realization that one's inner, vague intimations, now objectified in stone, are being expressed. For the contemporary spectator or average westernized tourist, since the response is not limited to an intellectual understanding alone, the genuine connection becomes a total experience, involving the artist and viewer in their common life processes on all levels. The work of sculpture mediates the relationship.

By entering the cave, the visitor becomes a participant in the physical forces operating amongst the space, columns and panels in an elaborate multiplication of interacting phenomena. The individual visitor to the cave is himself a closed/open system which coordinates balance, weight, motion, and relationship to gravity; therefore his presence in the spaces of the cave, within a magnetic field, is an additional system to be integrated into a relationship with all the other operating forces.

Systems

The pattern of organization of any system is the interpenetration of the components of the system. Essential to the sculptural system is the way in which the elements are configured. It is the synthesis of conjoined patterns, structure and the vital life of forms, an integrated whole whose essential properties arise from the relationships of its parts, and it is larger than the sum of its parts. In the system, different kinds of laws operate at different levels of complexity: tectonic processes, oppositions, resistances, counteractions are involved in a network with balance, rhythm, closure, harmonious tendencies and more.

The caves at Ellora are embedded in the solid mountain; the temples exist within the living space which surmounts the earth and interacts with planetary bodies and on and on in participation within galactic universes. This was understood by ancient Indian philosophers and master architects who were responsible for creating the systems, and it was very much felt by the average worshipper.

The traditional statue should be understood as being a single system, unique unto itself; at the same time it is an element existing within a complex of interacting systems – the cave and structural temples. While maintaining its individuality and its borders, and while it does have a lone presence, nevertheless it never stands alone, as it simultaneously becomes part of a perpetually expanding, larger complex. Only in the shrine is the idol separated; but it too, being itself a whole system, assumes a mobile place in the totality.

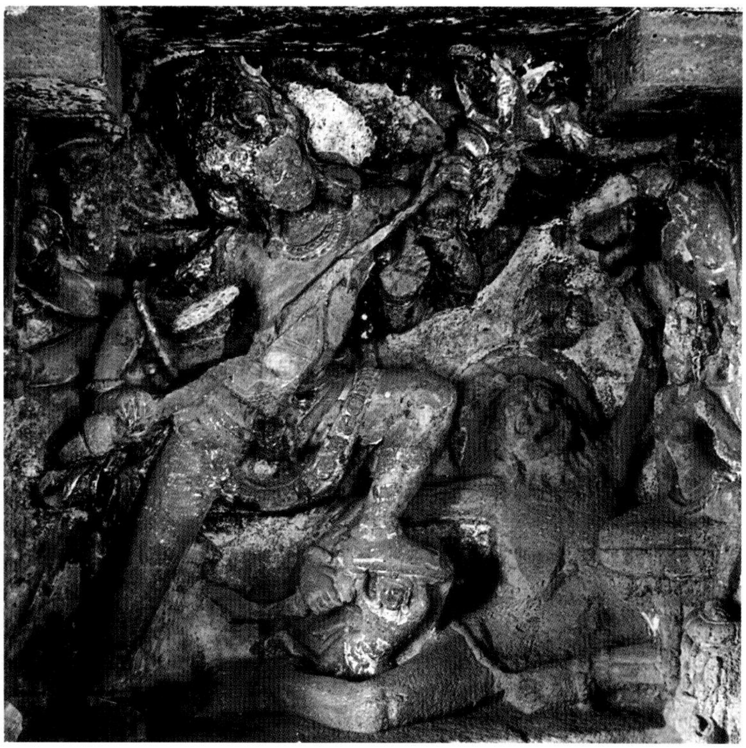

Fig. 6: **All the forms in active interrelationship are integrated into a system**

Andhakasura, Dasavatara, Cave 15, Ellora, Maharashtra, 8th c. C.E.

In the great sculptures, a single element contains potential for connecting with one or more of the remaining elements, so that the sculpture becomes a field of perpetually energized, interacting, interconnected forces, finally stabilized as a totality. Hopefully, when a spectator is in active participation with the sculpture, the operating forces will become evident at an intuitive level. Whether or not there is a non-material force, or whether all dynamism is a result of the interplay of forms as perceived by the spectator, what is important is to recognize the systems in perpetual interplay.

As we are concerned with systems, it might be useful to consider how all the caves at Ellora are integrated as systems within systems. A spectator can choose to focus on any small detail in a single panel, for example in Dasavatara, Cave 15. In the Andhakasura panel (Fig. 6), Siva's headdress (*makuta*) will do. As node, the *makuta* leads the eye in many directions, beyond the figure of Siva, but at the same time, it is recognizable as a form integral to Siva's own figure. The thrust of the figure is a directional sign, pointing towards the outside of the panel into space, while at the same time, it is one of the basic solids which is fixed firmly as an element of the framed system. And so on. How these complexities are perceived will depend on the spectator's ability and will to initiate the process of coming to grips with the interrelationships. Panel, spectator and the space between are operating within a magnetic field.

Some clues for becoming involved in the process can be noted in Dasavatara, Cave 15. Each individual figure within the framed panel is a bounded system. The framed panel is a system, and there are others: the many other framed panels and their individual forms, columns in the cave and their interconnections to each other and to the spaces in the aisles they create. The *vastupurusamandala* and its central point on the floor of the cave can be seen in connection with the other systems and with the landscape outside the cave and onward, to begin the grand endeavour of achieving intuitions concerning one's role and interconnection with the elements in the cave and in the interrelationships of the thirtyfour caves and their contents, surrounded by space, sky, mountain and geographical placement. There are infinite systems within systems within systems.

But in the final analysis, it is important to emphasize that pattern, structure and system, while essential to the underlying organization of the work, do not define the authentic work of art exclusively. Machines and the works of art that are subsumed by technology too are based on pattern, structure and are systems. What differentiates sculpture from machines is the life of form. This implies mobility and dynamic interaction of form life as differentiated from any mechanical static organization. I wrote about this in my book *The Life of Form in Indian Sculpture*. Therefore I will not refer to form life here. I only wish to lay emphasis on the fact that when the sculptor's instinctive life force with which he imbues the work is suppressed and is dominated by technology, which co-opts these instincts for itself, separating art from its reliance on living form, we, the artists, are in danger of ourselves becoming virtual. A theory of aesthetics which ignores this cannot be entirely valid.

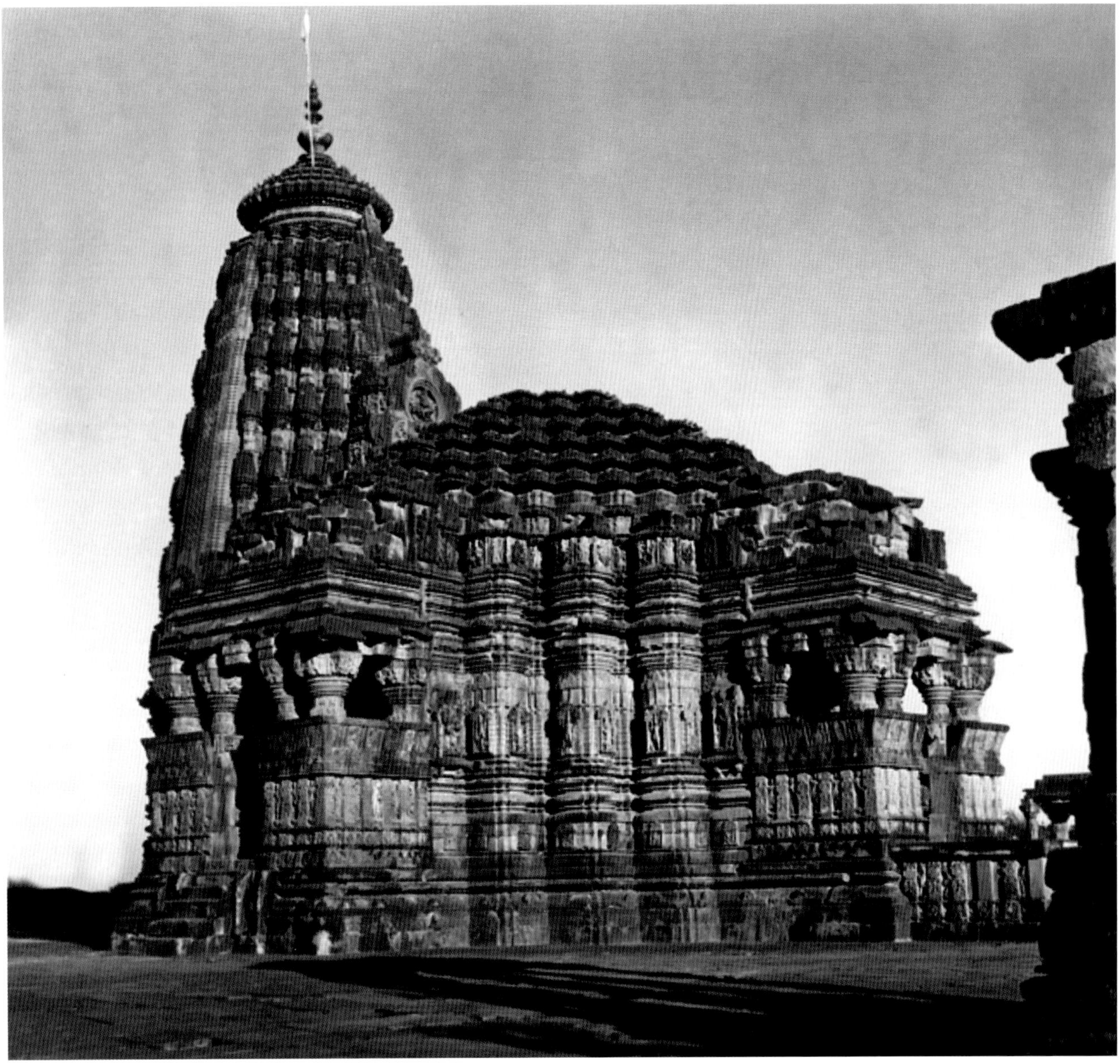

Fig. 7: **The Hindu temple is an integrated system, a synthesis of conjoined patterns, structures and the vital life of forms**

Nilakantesvara Temple,
Udayapur,
Madhya Pradesh, 11th c. C.E.

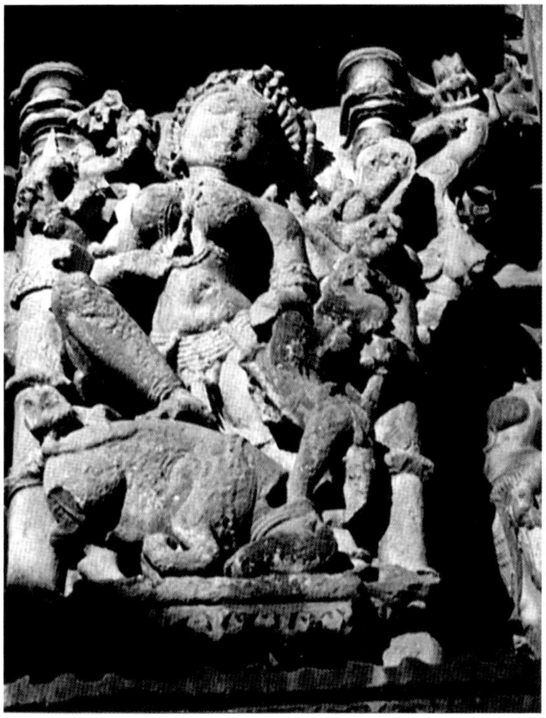

Fig. 8: **One system as part of the whole** Mahishamardini, Nilakantesvara Temple, Udayapur, Madhya Pradesh, 11th c. C.E.

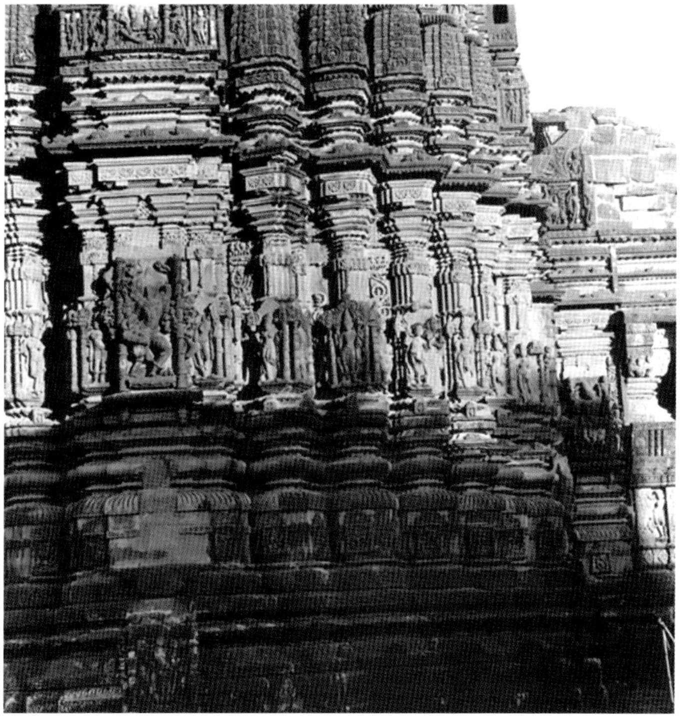

Fig. 9: **Systems are interrelated** Wall, partial view, Nilakantesvara Temple, Udayapur, Madhya Pradesh, 11th c. C.E.

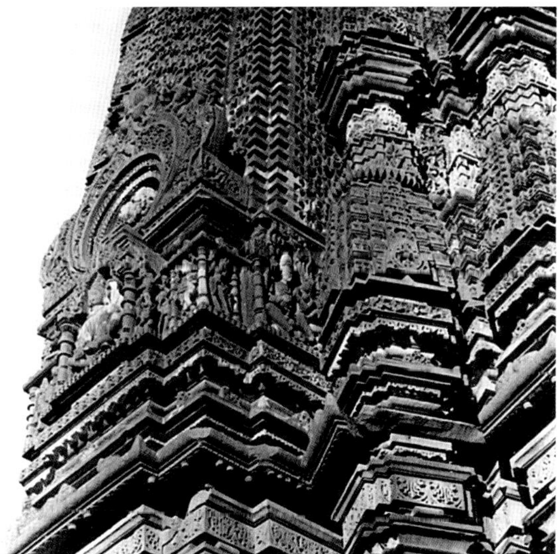

Fig. 10: **Systems are interrelated** *Sikhara*, partial view, Nilakantesvara Temple, Udayapur, Madhya Pradesh, 11th c. C.E.

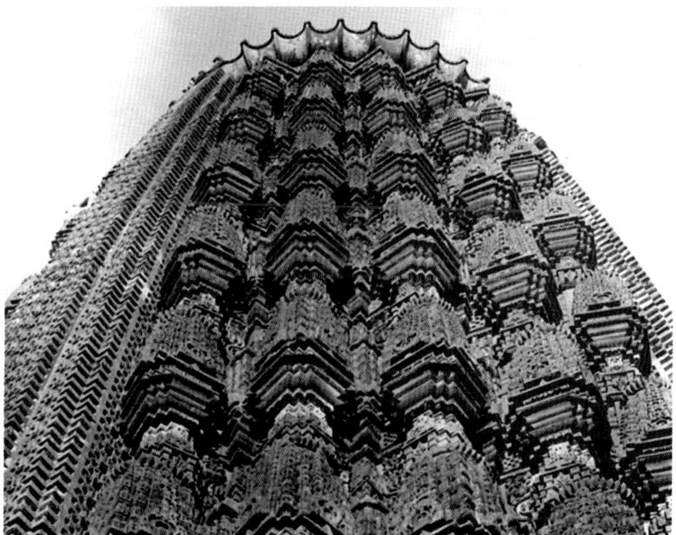

Fig. 11: **Systems are interrelated** *Sikhara*, partial view, Nilakantesvara Temple, Udayapur, Madhya Pradesh, 11th c. C.E.

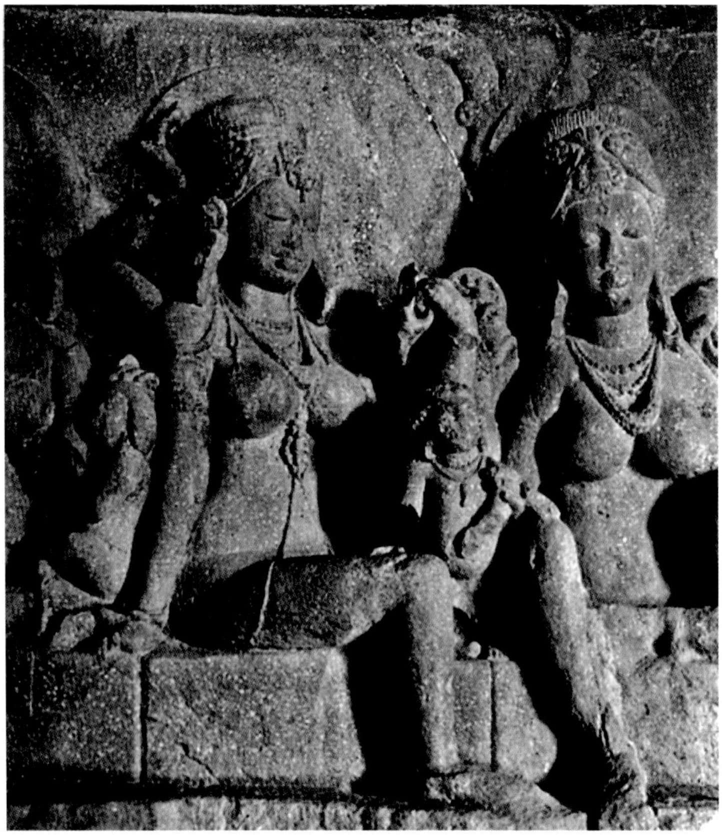

Fig. 12: **Youth in all its sensuality**

Sapta Matrika,
Ramesvara, Cave 21, Ellora,
Maharashtra, 6th c. C.E.

Fig. 13: **Upright, strict verticality**

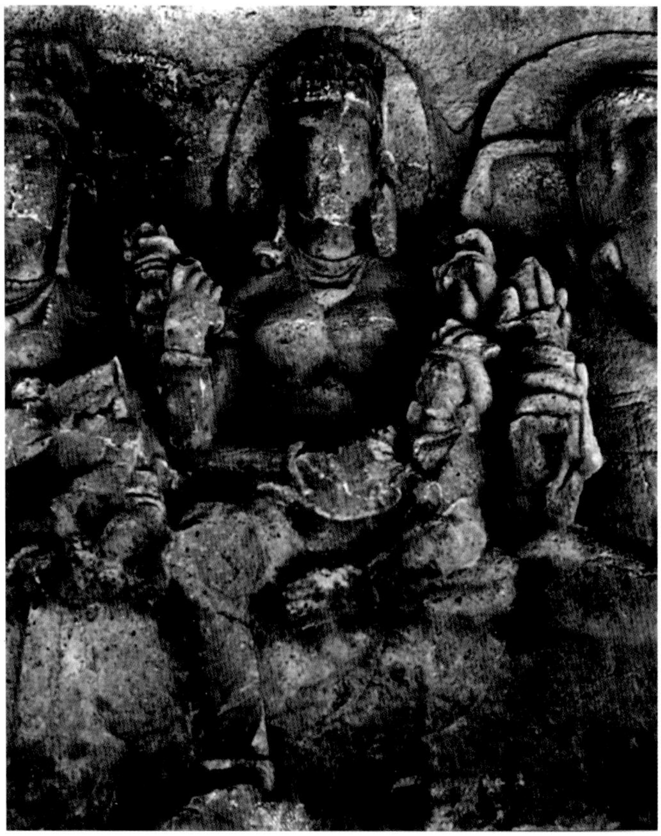

Sapta Matrika,
Ravana-ki-kai, Cave 14, Ellora,
Maharashtra, 7th c. C.E.

Contents

Previously, iconography, which was the knowledge recognized by members of a particular culture, had traditionally informed certain formal properties with conventional signification; the spectator had already been trained to recognize complex sets of relationships and the stock configuration of elements particular to that culture, although changes in styles often might have been confusing. Each specific system – the statue or group of statues – referred to a particular mythological concept which generally was familiar to the worshipper/spectator.

Today, while intrusive factors have transformed responses, imagery of divinities and the myriad mythical populations are present in the unconscious mind of most Indians, and although greatly compromised, still they are available for visual contact during daily encounters all about. The task for the contemporary visitors is to figure out how to recognize the particular narrative portrayed in the statues in the caves and temples (and in my own statues). But the average Indian today is generally unconcerned with naming the idol; people invest a particular idol with the name of their own chosen deity, and there are thousands of such appellations. If the worshipper is involved in a ritual directed towards a specific divinity, he will keep the name of the deity in mind. And if he is still in connection with the traditional lore as textually inscribed iconography, or should he be instructed by guides, art historians and students, he will enjoy participation in the cultural memory. Then he will be able to coordinate pattern and structure of interacting forms with content.

In a traditional society or even today, the ultimate truth is that god is unfathomable; the statue is merely something concretized as object for contemplation. Stones, trees, crudely made village idols or even random objects are actually equally appropriate objects of worship for a great majority of Indians. Various areas in India have specifically recognized deities, for example, Khandoba in central Maharashtra, but although often it is not easy to elicit standard answers to queries about the specific names, people do have the need to name their own particular deity.

What *is* possible is to elaborate on the relationship of form to content in the sculpture on temple walls and in the caves (and my own). Meaning is often implicit in content, and content is embodied in form. Forms are the signifiers beyond themselves. For example, Siva's dance is exhibited either as a vertically oriented, balanced, serene, supra-temporal event in Cave 21 (Fig. 4) or in Caves 15 (Fig. 5) and 16 in Ellora, it is aligned along extreme diagonals of the *panjara* to depict the great turbulence of the processes of creation, preservation and destruction. The *Sapta Matrikas* in Cave 21 (Fig. 12) are youth in all its fulsome sensuality; here basic shapes rely on sphere and oval, while in Cave 14 (Fig. 13), their upright, strict verticality tells of their disciplined aspect. Which emphasis the sculptor will choose will determine how content can be recognized in form.

As Lévi-Strauss has emphasized, many people come to the system they want to study with preconceived ideas about what they are looking at; there can be little understanding. So, when entering a cave or gallery, it is useful to approach the representations of culturally diverse works of art with an open mind, to be ready to begin the voyage of exploration.

SECTION III

Sculpture: Diagrams of Immanent Underlying Patterns

Carmel Berkson

Dasavatara, Cave 15, Ellora

In a positive stance, I joyfully and gratefully place myself on the side of the history of sculpture. Should the sculptor identify herself with the myth, the divinities, the aesthetics, with the stone and space and with the long historical, cultural and religious background, she may rediscover her real self. Rather than putting our head in the sand and denying history, if we are genuinely committed to a true aesthetic experience and a broader grasp of the human condition, so that we can better cope with modern society, we can take courage from past glories. Reconnecting with resources left to us by the great master architects and sculptors here in India would seem to be the wiser choice. As a reaction against how technology has been imposed upon life, we crave the organic and the beautiful in sculpture even more desperately. Once universal qualities in art are understood and incorporated into our response systems, art can play a crucial role in an effort to heal a sorrowing world.

Whether or not there is order or chaos at a quantum level, and even while everything in the temporal world is in continuous transformation, fragmentation of our daily lives disrupts the fixed and immutable factors of our inner world. At the deeper levels of the human psyche, there always is a fundamental need, desire and tendency to be in connection with an indivisible totality, beyond individuation and contingencies.

Because I recognized affinities with the statues I had made prior to my arrival in India, my first encounter with the sculpture of India was an immediate sense of connection, and I reacted at a deep, instinctual level. The immanent pattern and the underlying interactivity of the basic shapes was familiar to me, because as a self-trained sculptor, when I was first learning to manipulate the clay and to invest it with content, these elemental processes automatically came to be inherent in my early statues. Even though I had had no idea of an underlying diagram, the pattern had emerged out of my conscious/unconscious processing (Figs. 14a, b, c). I now understand this response as a product of the functioning of brain/mind. To elaborate on these fundamentals and to organize the work into a totality of its interpenetrating parts and to invest the forms with life has been the task of years.

So when I was first in the presence of the *Siva Dancing in Lalita* at Elephanta, I experienced a wonderful aesthetic shock. This is the response which surpasses individual identity, which an aware worshipper/spectator will have as she confronts a great work of art. Without thought, perception of the patterns underlying the complex structure of form-life happens spontaneously, preceding the immediate mental identification. I searched India for more such revelations, and everywhere I went, I discovered the ubiquity of the *panjara*, of structure and of the interacting life of form on the structural temples and the cave temples (Figs. 15-20 – a, b, c), which the following diagrams will illustrate.

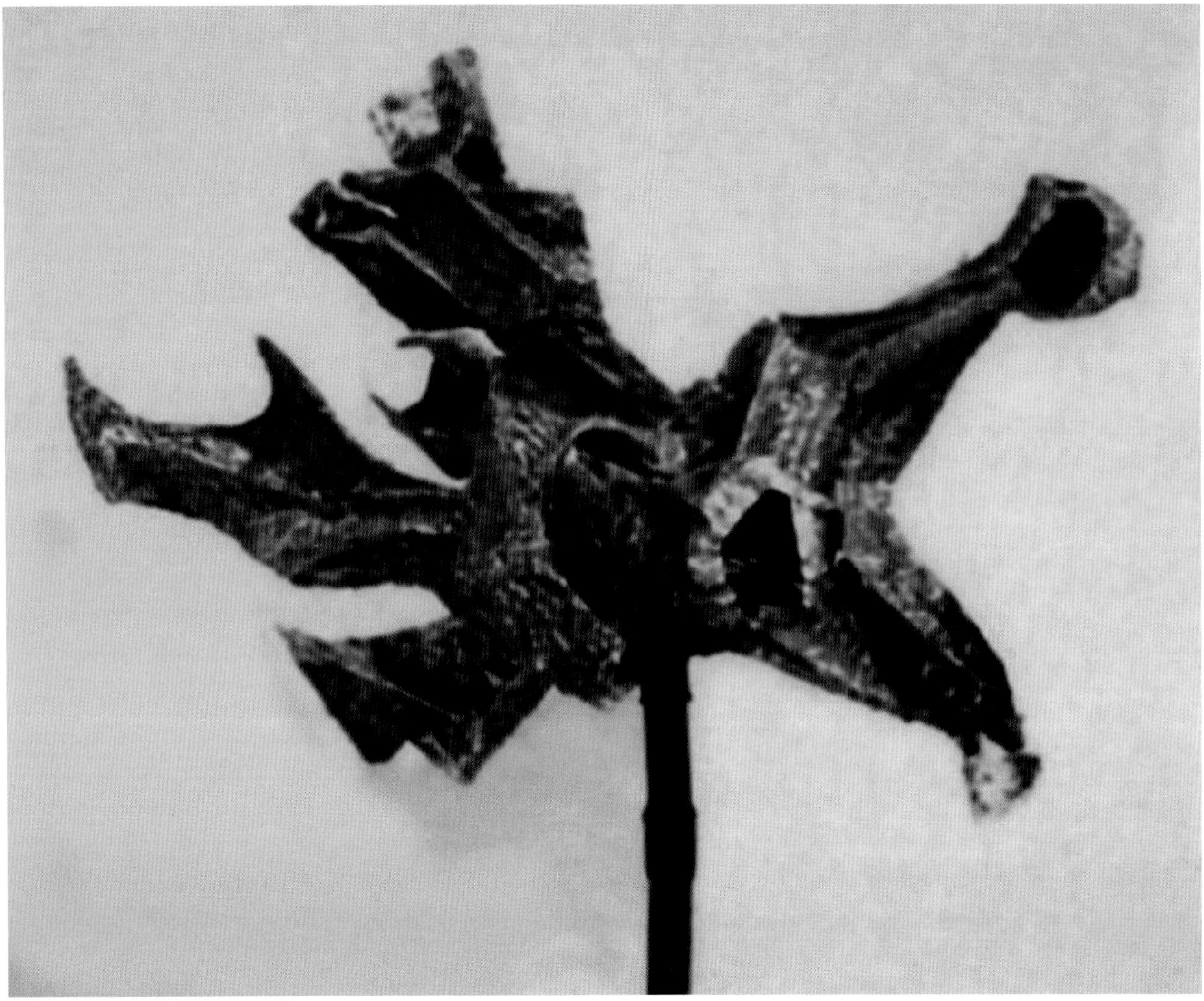

Fig. 14a: **Even though I had no idea of an underlying diagram, the pattern had emerged out of my conscious-unconscious processing**

Carmel Berkson, Untitled
Welded copper sheet, 2½' x 1' (1965)

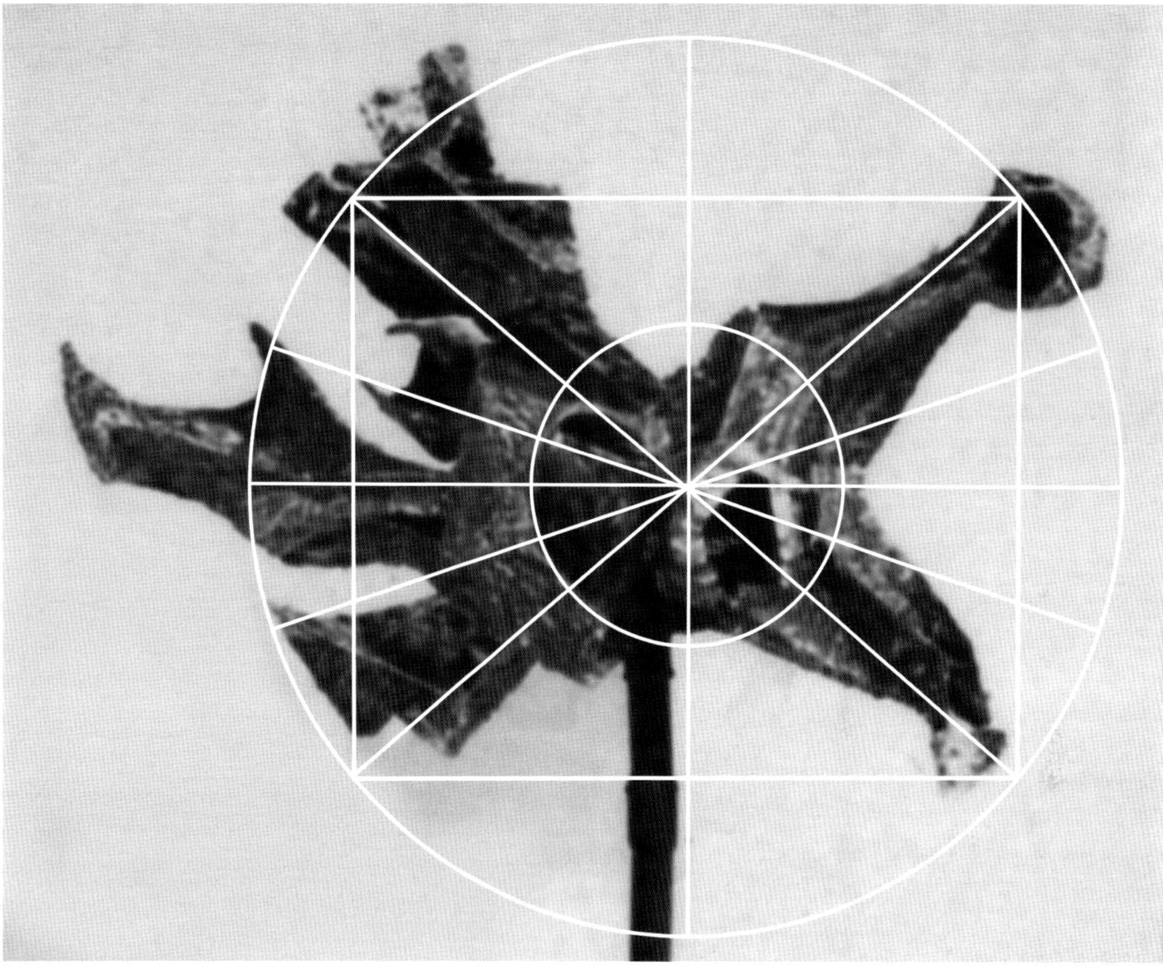

Fig. 14b

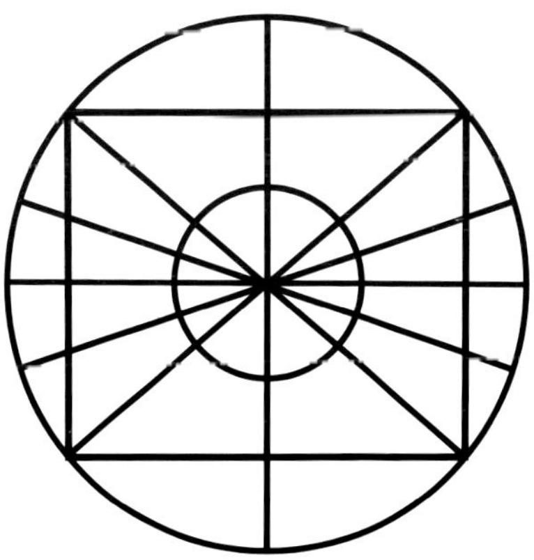

Fig. 14c

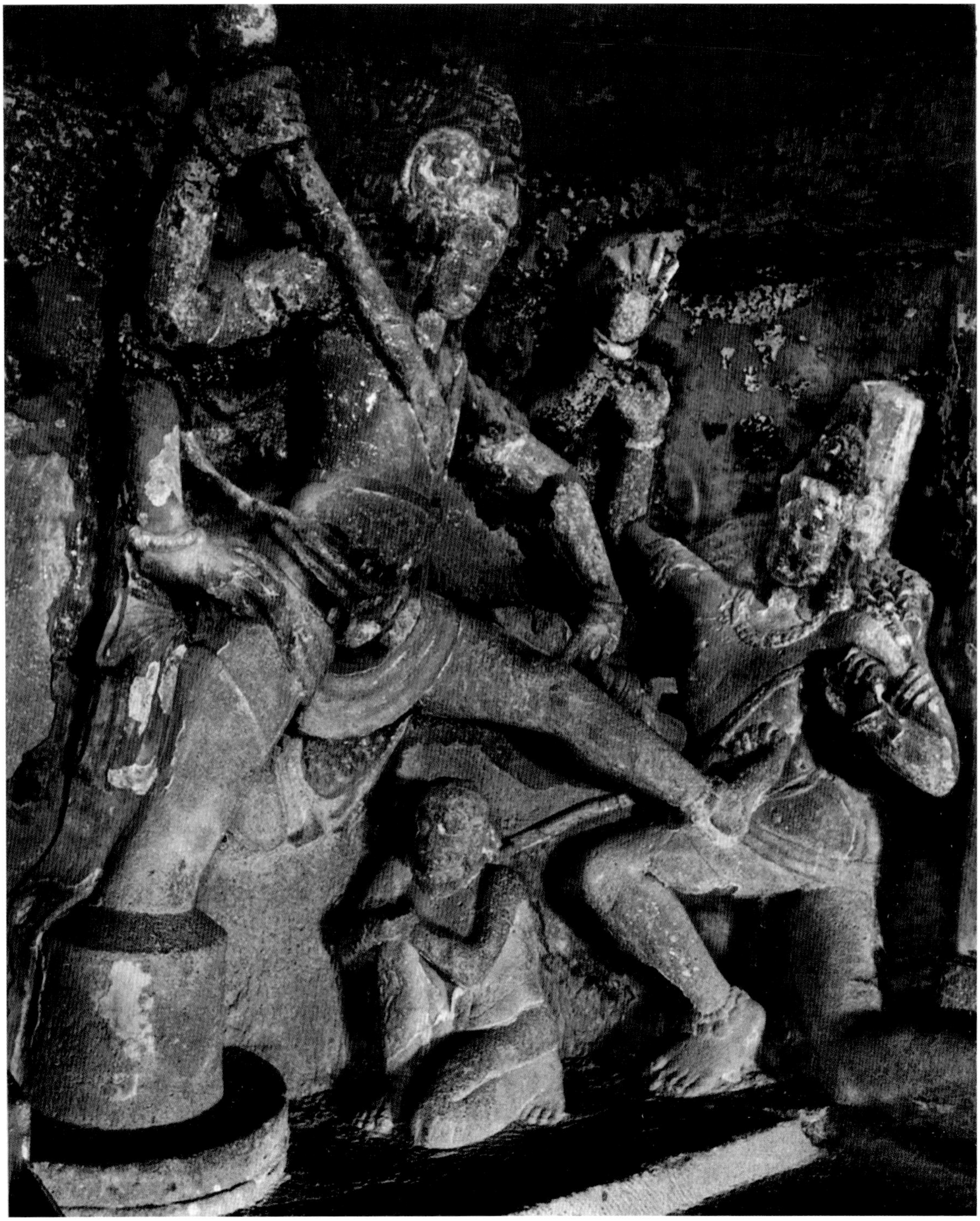

Fig. 15a: **Pattern, structure, system**

Siva as Kala – Kala, the Destroyer of Death,
Dasavatara, Cave 15, Ellora,
Maharashtra, 8th c. C.E.

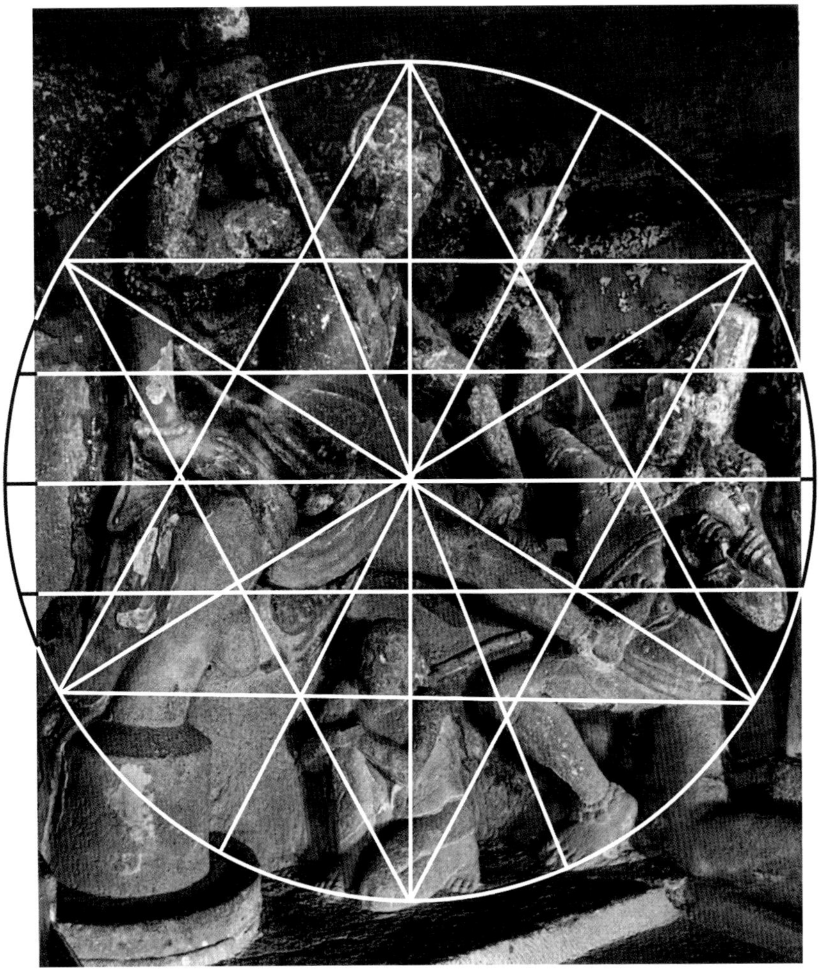

Fig. 15b

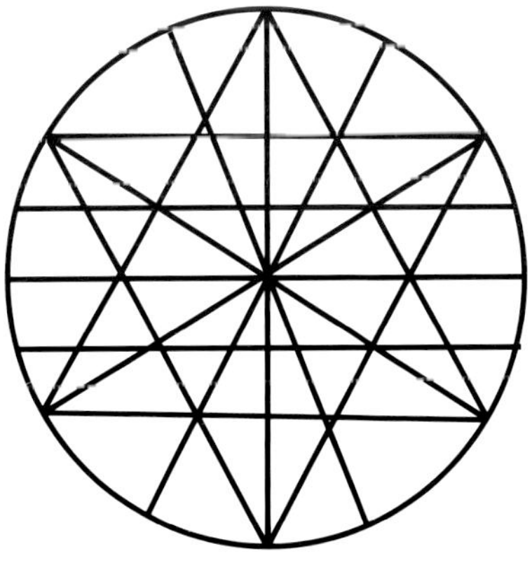

Fig. 15c

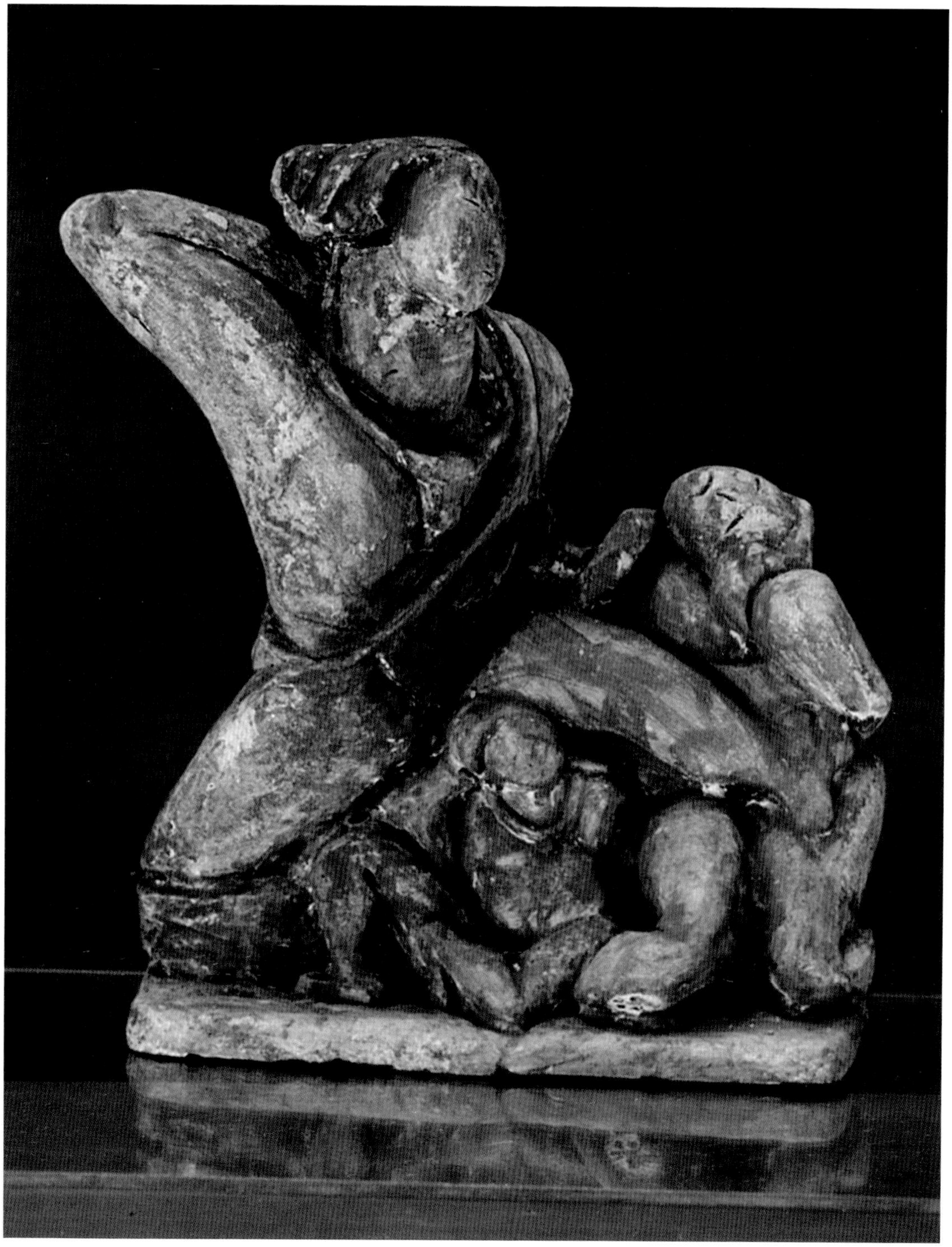

Fig. 16a: **Pattern, structure, system**

Siva as Kala – Kala, the Destroyer of Death,
Carmel Berkson,
Bronze, 10½" x 7½" x 14"

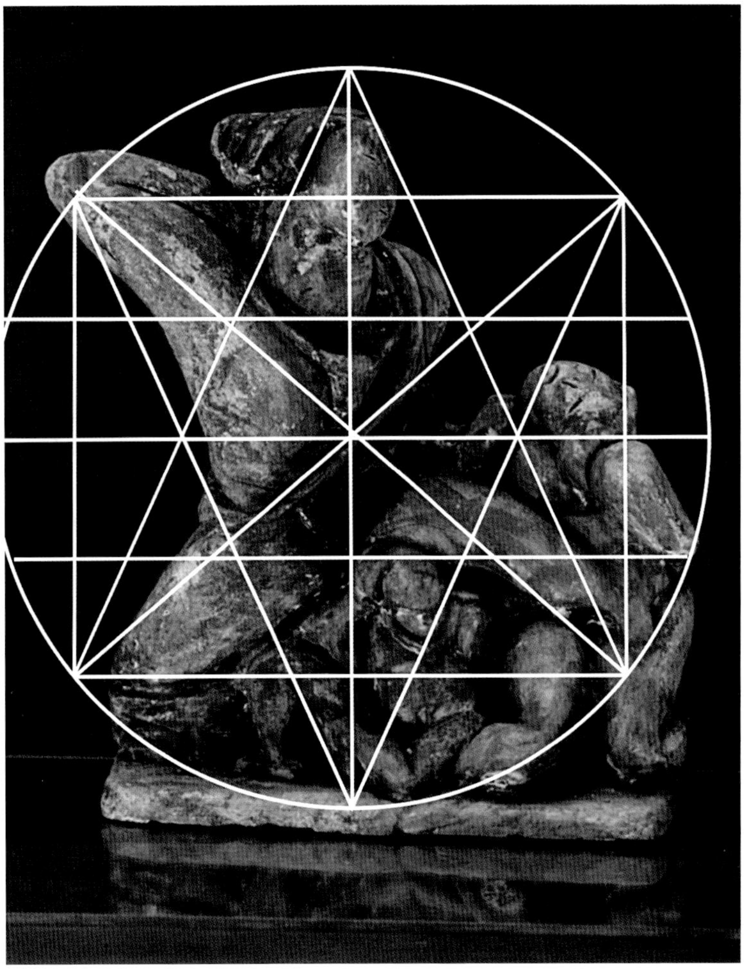

Fig. 16b

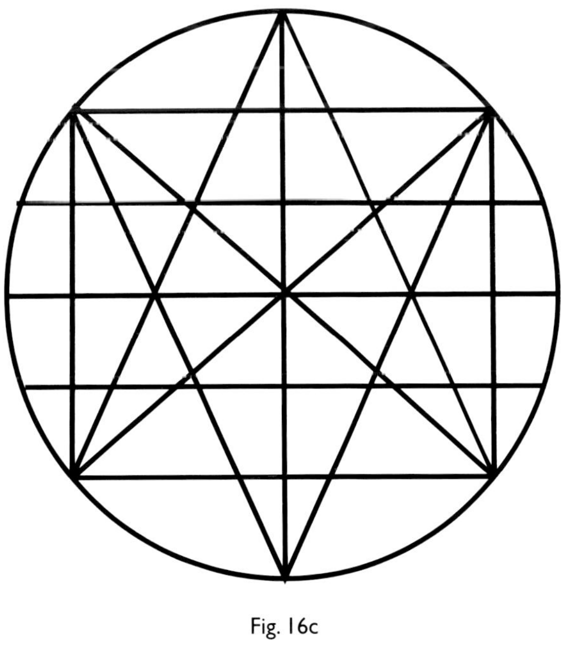

Fig. 16c

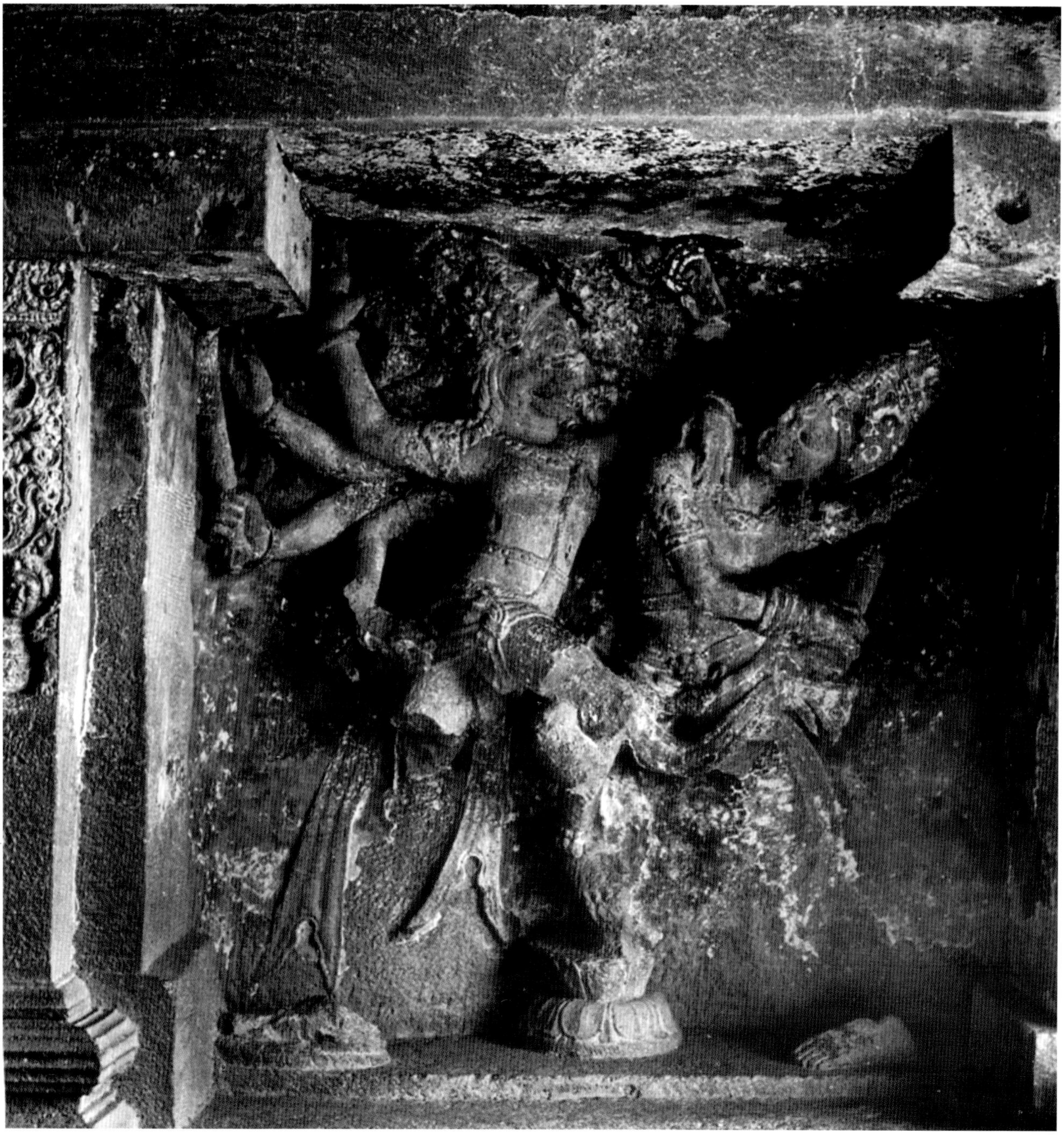

Fig. 17a: **Pattern, structure, system**

Narasimha/Hiranyakasipu,
Dasavatara, Cave 15, Ellora,
Maharashtra, 8th c. C.E.

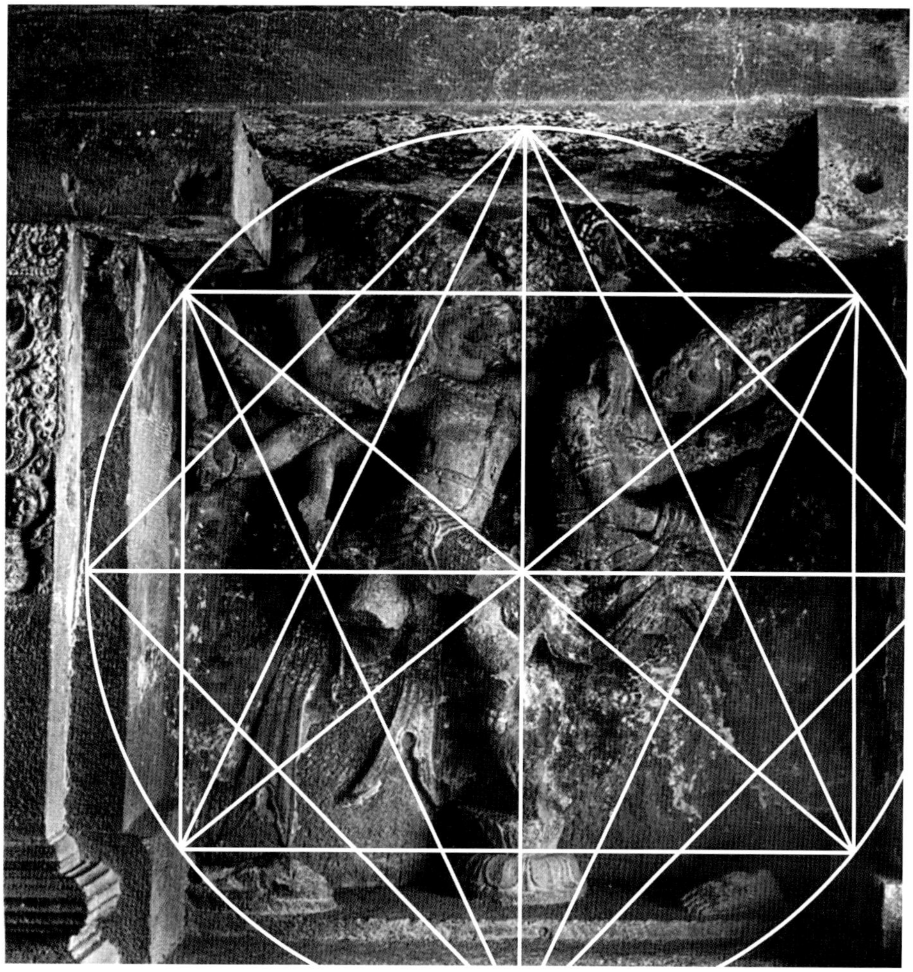

Fig. 17b

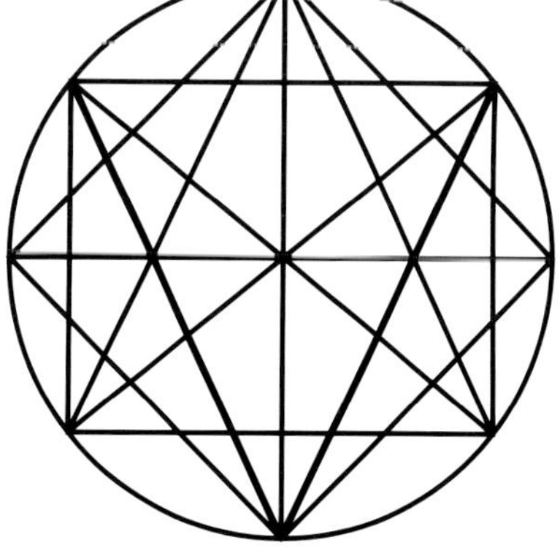

Fig. 17c

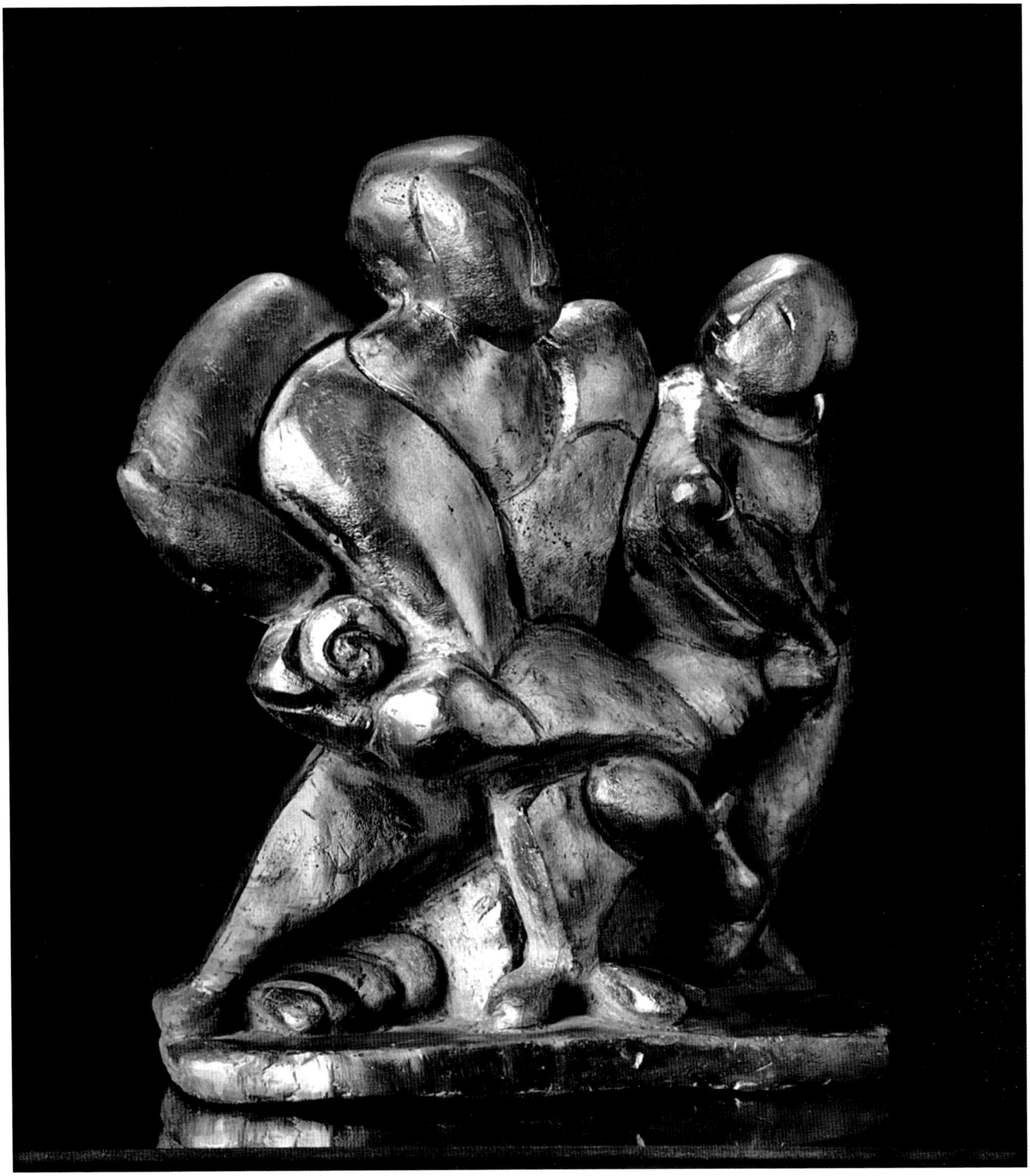

Fig. 18a: **Pattern, structure, system**

Narasimha/Hiranyakasipu,
Carmel Berkson,
Bronze, 12" x 7" x 15"

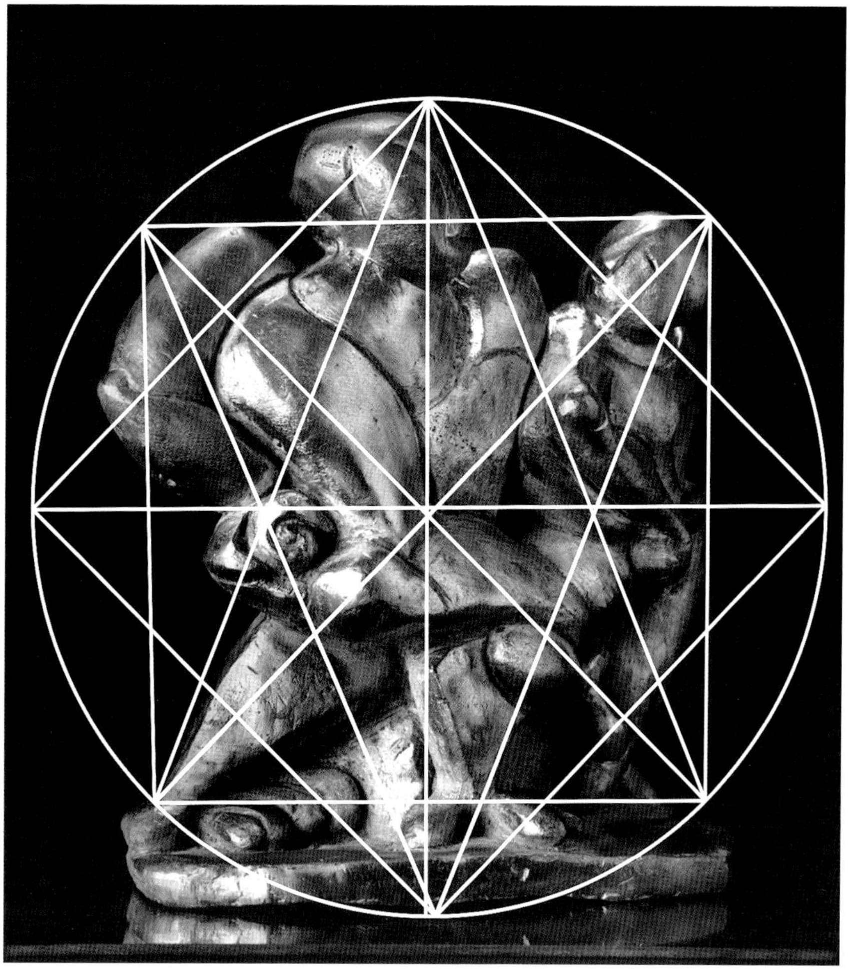

Fig. 18b

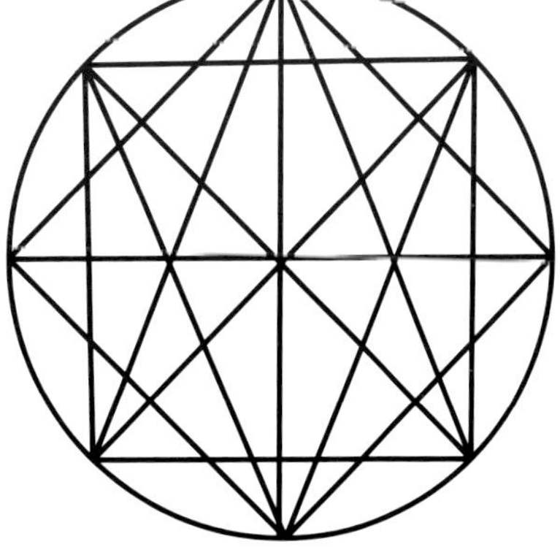

Fig. 18c

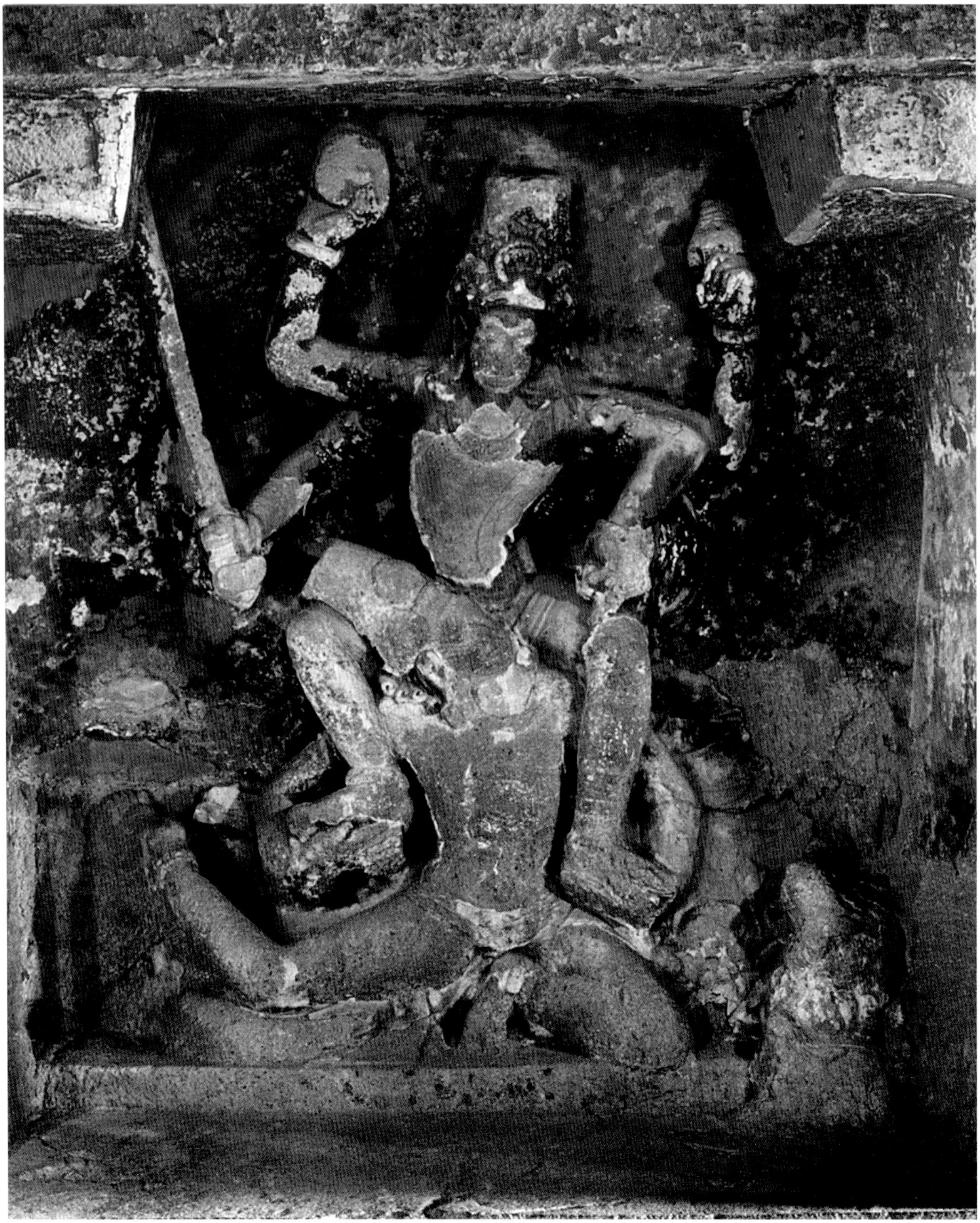

Fig. 19a: **Pattern, structure, system**

Gajendramoksha,
Dasavatara, Cave 15, Ellora,
Maharashtra, 8th c. C.E.

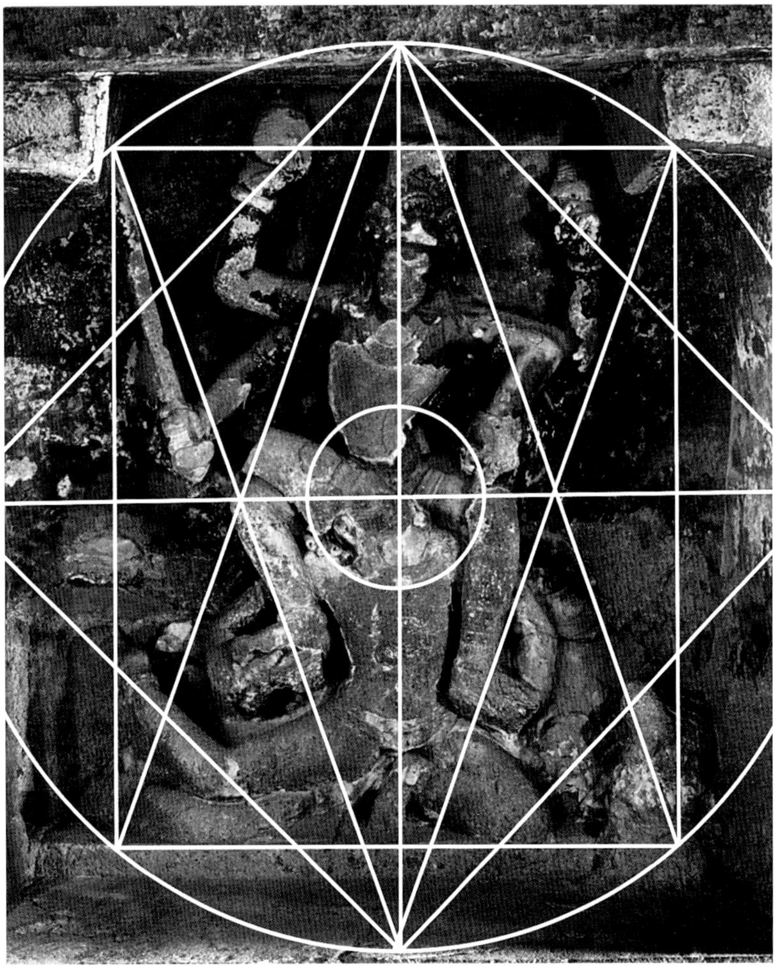

Fig. 19b

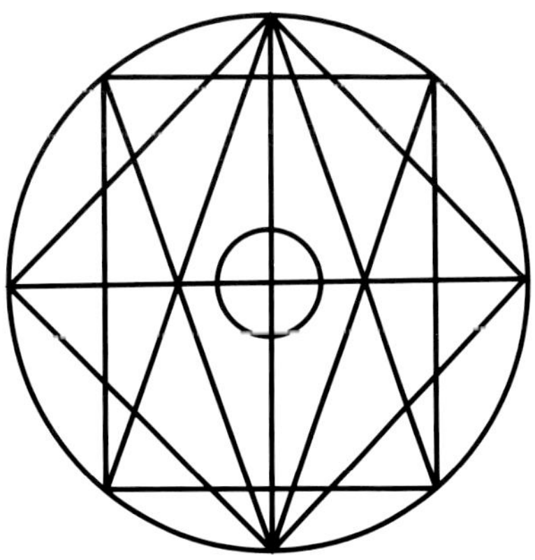

Fig. 19c

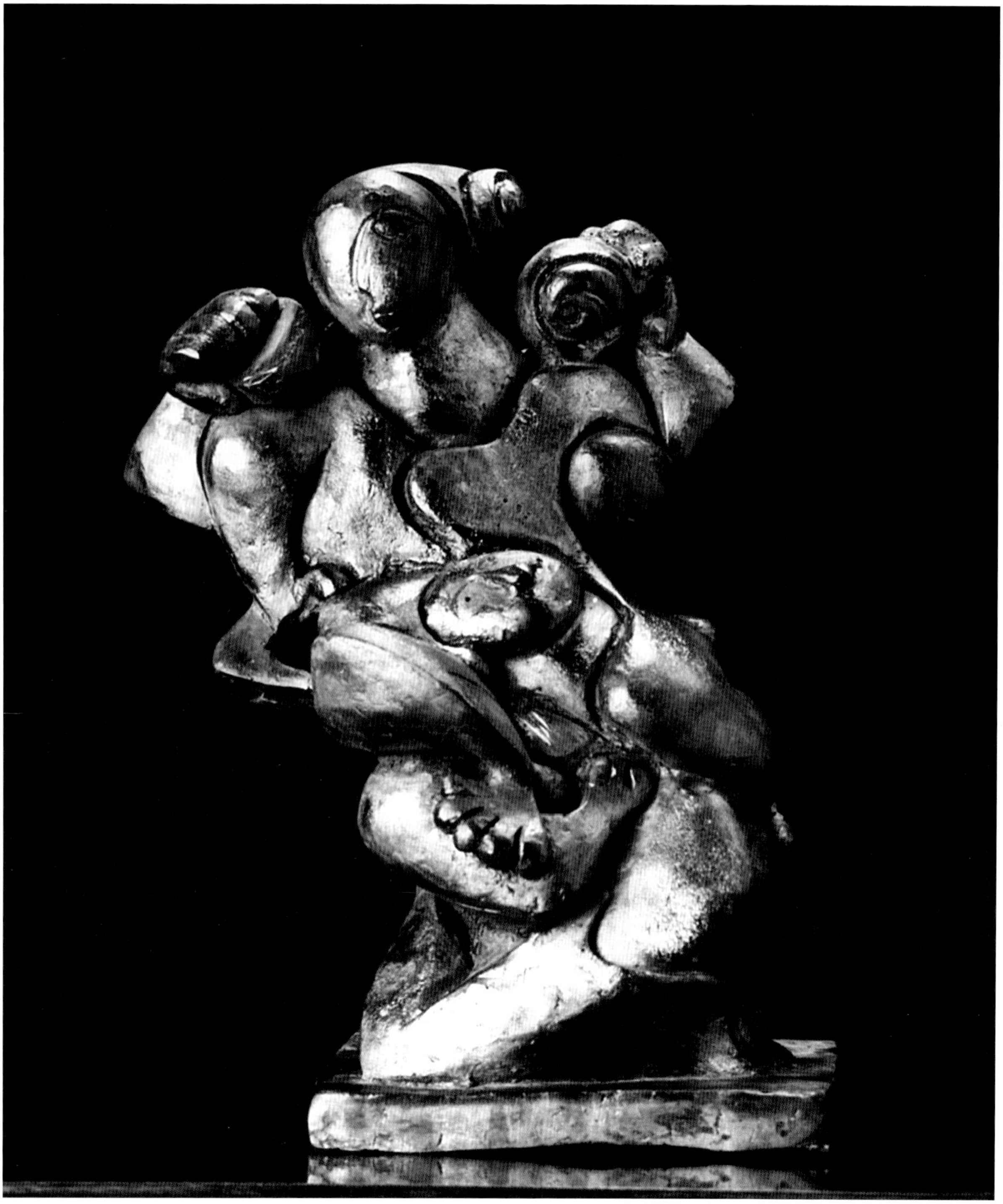

Fig. 20a: **Pattern, structure, system**

Gajendramoksha,
Carmel Berkson,
Bronze, 12" x 9" x 9"

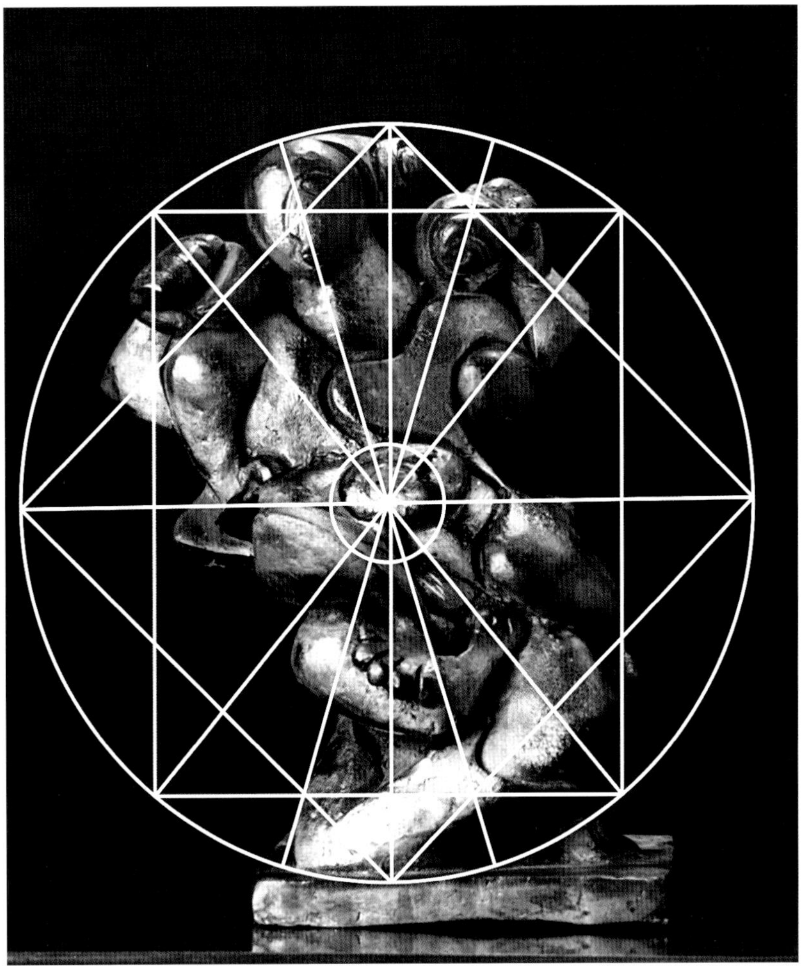

Fig. 20b

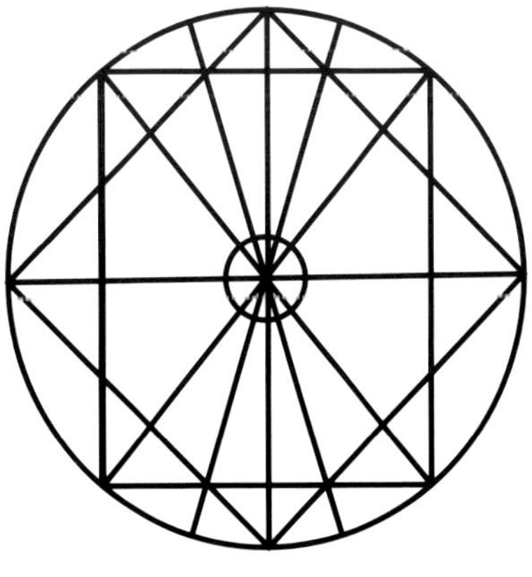

Fig. 20c

I have always maintained that the photographs are merely an introduction, and that the only way really to know any sculpture is to be in physical contact within the space surround. Verbal explanations are merely introductory. Perceiving involves the spectator in a process which might be defined as the coordination of all the properties of the statue and of the life of the perceiver. And my books have been invitations for people to come to the temples for the true experience. But as a prior effort, it might be possible to talk about what one can look for – or I should say, what one can become involved in – when one is in contact with my own statues.

Life of form

As we have defined the pattern and structure, we should consider what gives the impression of energy when in actuality we are in the presence of non-living matter. There is life in forms, or forms are in life. The elements in the statue are basic shapes having their origin in three-dimensional geometry – cylinder, sphere, ovoid, block or pyramid. These vary in scale, thickness, in how much they deviate from pure geometry, how the sculptor, in his infinite discrimination, moulds the original form into unique, organic shapes distributed in relation to variations in proximity with others and to projections and recessions of the depth of the various planes. I try to create a work where the parts are coordinated into an energized field. Outlines of the shapes, the spaces amongst the shapes, light reflected on projections and absorbed in the voids will also be integrated into the whole. There are infinite possibilities as to in what way all this is effected.

The goal is to create a whole system, the components of which are in vital, complex, interconnections. While locked within a closed structure, energies are simultaneously forced outward. As we have seen, the *panjara* emits its energies from the centre; these energies are confined within the circumference, effecting a continuous oscillation between *bindu* and outer circle. Each statue should be a living field with forces operating from within. I try to respect these forces and be guided by them so that the statue never sinks into static banality. Implied in the *panjara's* internal forces is the Sanskrit meaning of the word – it refers to a caged lion; this implies the intensity of these oscillations – the tighter they are compressed, the more interpenetration of all the elements in the statue, the more powerful will be the confrontation.

A perceptive viewer will differentiate between a quiet composition and one that is a cauldron of interacting, opposing and reciprocal forces. Hopefully, the spectator will recognize the forms to be in mobile activity – a clash of counter-directional thrusts and torsions. If gravity dominates, there will be stasis; if there is too much similarity among the shapes, the statue will be lifeless. What is meant by the 'life of form' is the result of the efforts made to invest the statue or panel with movement and energy, to reflect the continuous dynamic activity of living species. Ultimately, while all is in mobile transformation, everything must come to be a whole, a totality larger than the combination of the parts. Once the tensions are accessed by the viewer, she can observe the complex oppositions operating within the structure: convergence/expansion; rhythm/dissonance; harmony/dynamic ambiguity; levitation/gravity; distortion/rest; mobility/stasis and so much more. These are our ideals. I can only make the attempt at partial achievement.

The transcendence of binary oppositions may be a concept with which to approach each of my chosen themes. As an example, I can cite the fact that, after Durga slays Mahisha, the buffalo demon, in the text he rises up to heaven and sits at her side. Or in another instance, after Siva slays the demon Andhakasura, the demon becomes a devotee of Siva. In the statues, although two figures are independent, they simultaneously are united in a unit which is larger than each of its parts. In the activity of the life of forms antagonism and attraction is implied and so is the transcendence.

The role of myth

I have learned about Indian symbolism with much appreciation of the role of myth and the conscious and unconscious predispositions in a traditional society. Most of my statues contain mythological references. When the cultural and religious background is understood, and when the title of my statues is read, the stories will hopefully add another element to the formal qualities in the aesthetics and will become integrated as one message. While the style is my own language, the message is transpersonal. Although most of my earlier sculpture was abstract, embodying the sculptural-structural relationships with the content of the myth was the natural result of living in India and having been immersed in the cultural paradigms.

When I make my statues, I have a mental connection, not with the myths of India only, but those that have analogies with other cultures as well. Most of the myths of India have familiar meanings and shouldn't be too remote from the viewer's collective unconscious understanding. In this century, and the last, we have been privileged to study all of world art; we have emerged out from the single viewed perspective. As we are learning more and more about the human brain, it is becoming easier to contact the underlying similarities in our various productions, even if we choose to represent only one particular culture. For example, Abraham is ready to sacrifice Isaac (Fig. 66); Wajashrawas sacrifices

Nachiketa (Figs. 67, 68). The power of the female is portrayed as the Amazon (Fig. 60) battles Theseus and Durga battles Mahisha (Figs. 24-31).

Rasa

The role of art is to reflect the many aspects of the human condition. Most of my statues allude to psychological states which are emotionally complex and are generally repressed. The statue will speak to the viewer to elicit recognition of a particular reality; recognitions will bring acceptance, relief, catharsis and an externalized emotional response. The statue must not be a realistic copy; it has only to refer to a concrete emotional state in order to contact the sufferer, the lover, he who longs or feels anger or he who feels any other of the emotional states. When he understands that his particular internal self (*atman*) is similar to others' and is being subtly accessed, he will thus be in empathetic alliance with the sculptor and will feel deep satisfaction and emotional peace, in fact, he will experience *ananda*.

In India, the empathetic reactivity between artist and perceiver is described as the result of the experience of *rasa*. The *rasa* theory defines nine major sentiments or states of mind. The word *rasa* has a variety of subtle meanings but might be generally understood as that essence or provocation of an emotional state that exists within the work of art which has the potential of being transferred to the *rasika*, he who is sensitive to what is being conveyed. As my statues are projections of my own states of mind, I do hope that it may be possible for some to become aware of the implicit emotional state (*rasa*).

To mention only a few statues: David and Absalom and Buddha with Dying Warrior might evoke *Karuna* (sorrow, compassion). *Yab-Yum*, Reclining Nude, Laksmi and Visnu as mare and horse portray *Shringara* (erotic love). *Raudra* (furious, angry) would describe Mahishamardini and the Amazon, while the Sacrifice of the First-Born relates to *Bhayanaka* (terrible, fear) (see pages 115-136).

SECTION IV

Carmel Berkson: Sculpture and Related Myths

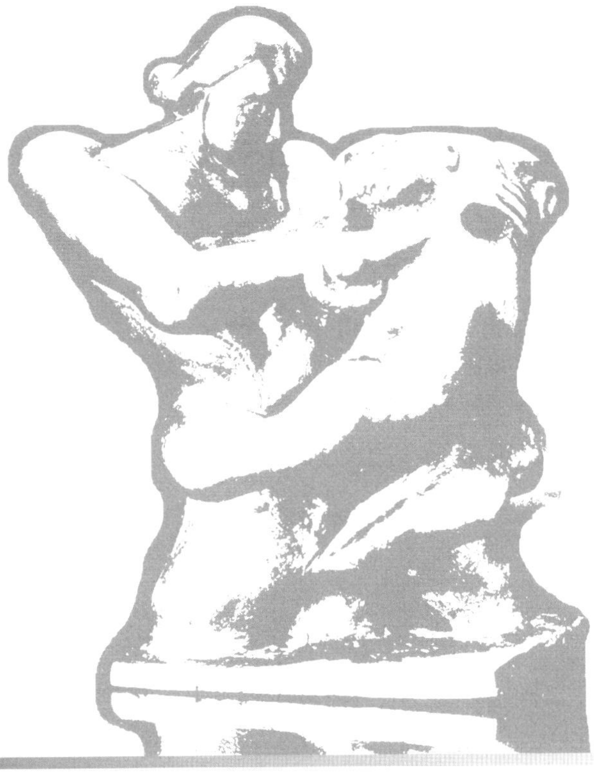

Indra

Indra-Vrtra Struggle
(Fig. 21)

The struggle between Indra and Vrtra exemplifies the paradigmatic demon/god oppositions so fundamental to Indian mythology. The narrative is first encountered in the Rig Veda. Perennially experiencing water as primal survival need in times of drought, the poets sang about the invincible demon Vrtra, who imprisoned the waters in the dark clouds. To the great distress of the people, Vrtra's swollen body retained all the waters of the universe.

Indra came to the rescue, having had his fill of Soma. A fierce, archetypal battle raged. "Then Heaven himself, the mighty, at that Dragon's roar, reeled back in terror, when Indra, in the wild joy of Soma, had struck off with might the head of Vrtra, the tyrant of earth and heavens. He rolled in the midst of never ceasing currents, flowing without a rest forever onward, causing floods to flow for man."[1]

Though separated by millennia, the fundamental theme of struggle is retained in the *Mahabharata* and later texts, but the focus on release from drought has been transformed into tales of fratricide, filicide and duplicity.

When threatened by the three-headed Trisiris, who had become very powerful, his brother Indra killed him, thus becoming a Brahmanicide. So the angry father Tvaster (*Visvakarma*) engendered another son, Vrtra, for the purpose of killing Indra.

Here the melding of themes from other accounts is evident. Vrtra attained the boon of invulnerability, but Indra ultimately did kill Vrtra, although the demon had hidden in a vast mountain of foam on the shores of the ocean. Sometimes, while Brahma is on the side of demons, a way to counter the god's powers is found. But the interactions of conflict and temporary resolutions endure.

Motifs

1. Nature personified
2. God/demon struggle
3. Fratricide, filicide
4. Power of austerities

---

[1]Rig Veda, Book I, LIII:8.

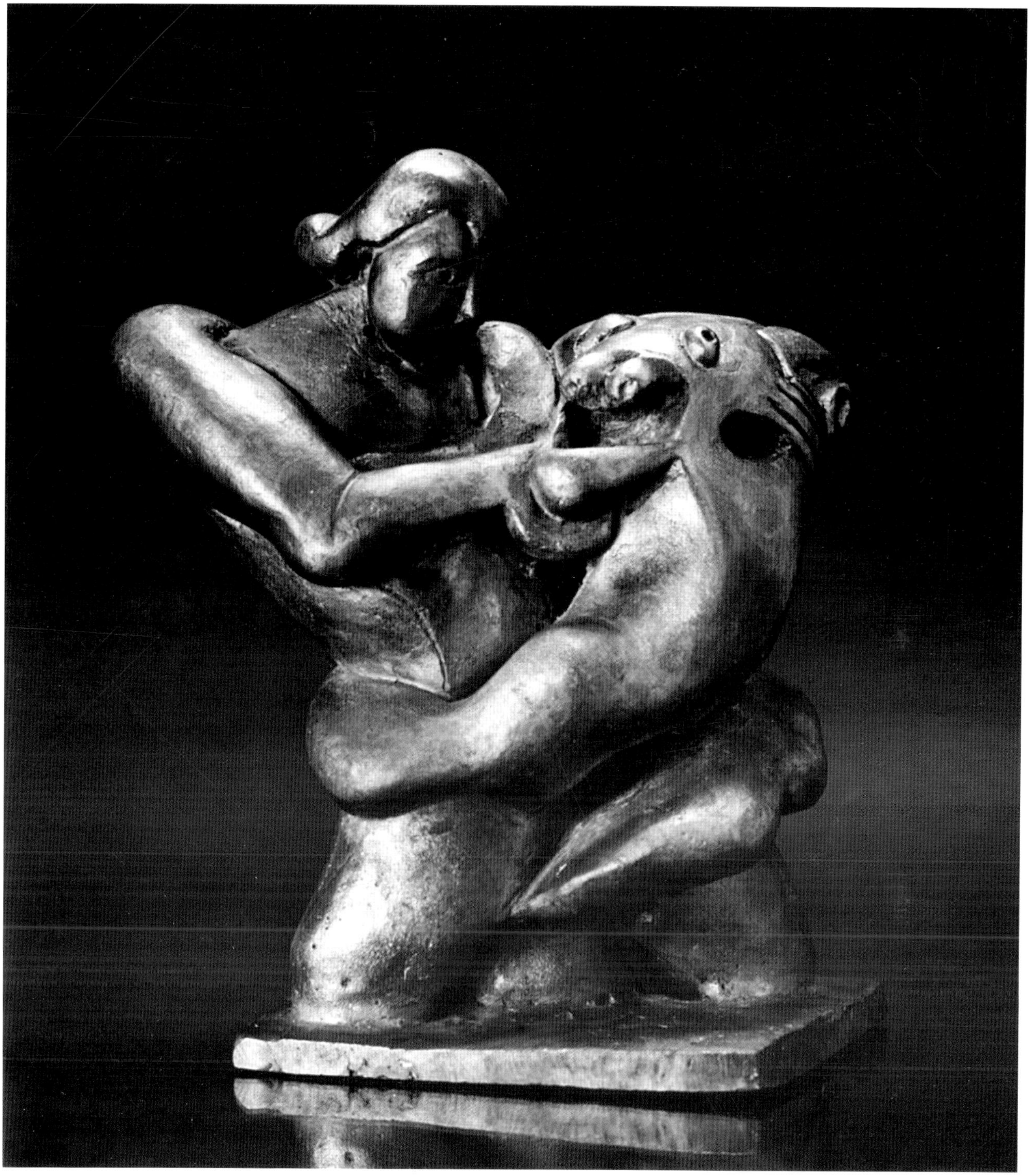

Fig. 21: **Indra Slays Vrtra**

Carmel Berkson,
Bronze, 7½" x 6½" x 13½"

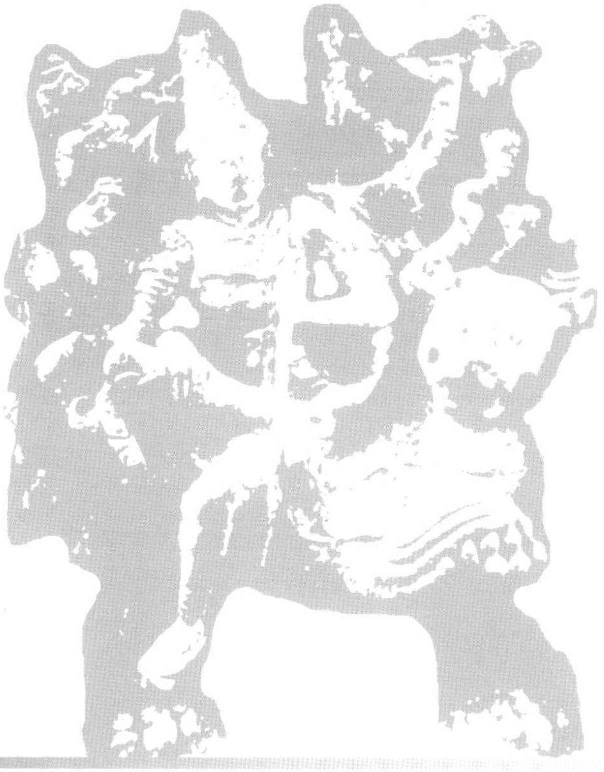

Durga on Lion

Durga on Lion
(Figs. 22-23)

The half human, half animal (buffalo or lion) female deity was only in later times split into two distinct components. Before that, human and animal were conceived as conjoined in the form of a single divine being. Later, throughout the vast area where the goddess reigned supreme – from the Mediterranean eastward to India and beyond – the ancient mistress of animals was depicted astride or in proximity with her erstwhile, inseparable, symbiotic partner. These connections have never been entirely severed. The potent female energy which had been the driving force for millennia was never abandoned by the Indian people. It was, and is, an independent, atavistic force, which still does dominate the consciousness of the captive devotees of the goddess. For the worshipper, the goddess symbolizes the power, strength, beauty, but also the frightening, destructive nature of her lion vehicle.

In Indian sculpture, although she also has other animal vehicles, the bellicose goddess Durga is often shown seated on the lion, and although she always has a benign expression on her face, and as in the case here depicted, the lion appears to be peaceful as well, the worshipper is aware that one can never predict the instantaneous transformations which characterize her uncountable, many moods. Contained in her are all aspects and possibilities of diverse human characteristics – from the ferocious to the sublime, from the horrific to the benign, and all intervening states. She has always been, and still is, the reigning, powerful, beloved/destroyer, as well as she who bestows bounties. She is the mother of all.

Motifs

1. Human/animal ambiguity
2. Constancy of responses during millennia
3. Divinity embodies human traits

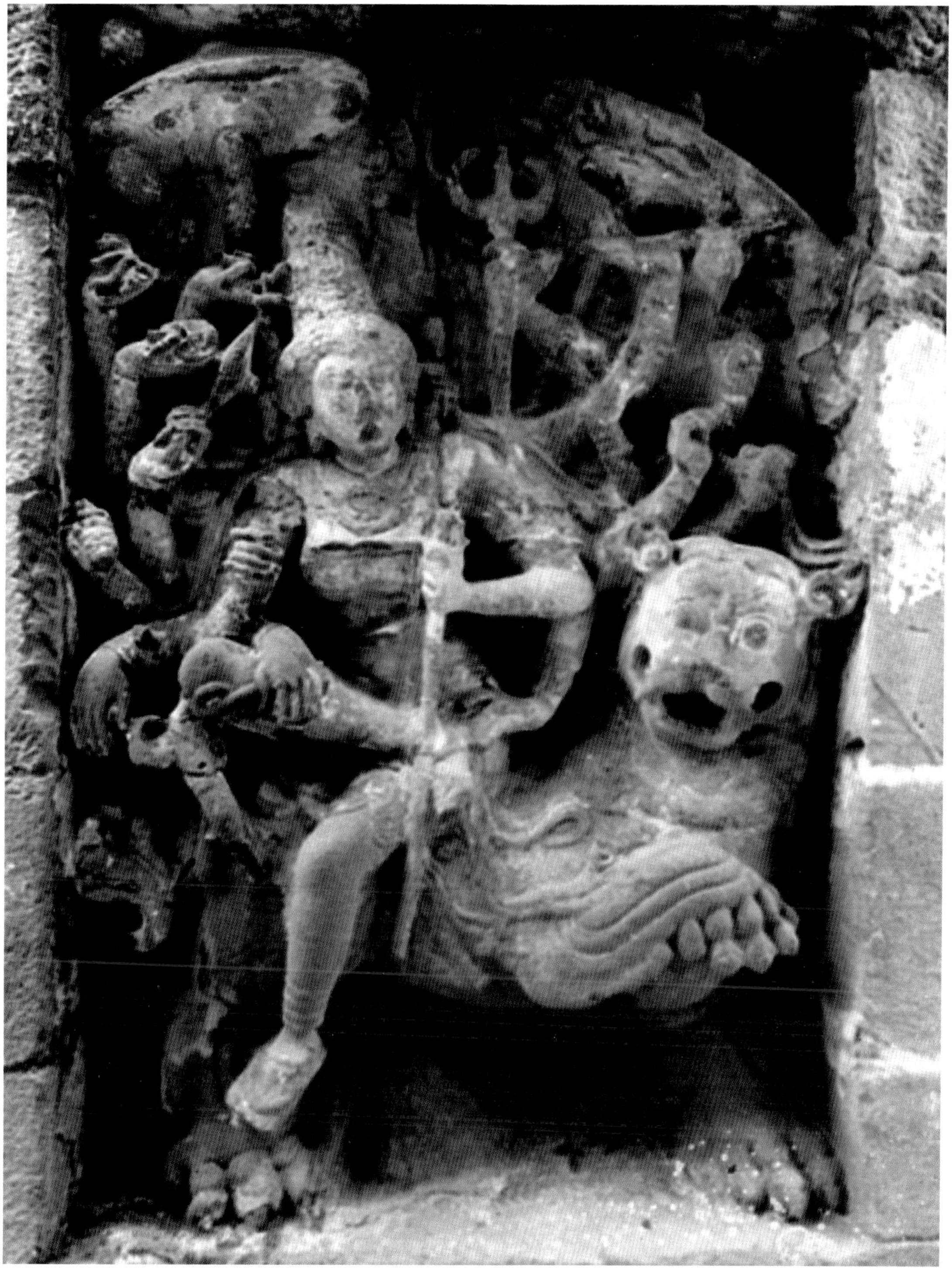

Fig. 22: **Durga on Lion**

Kailashnatha Temple,
Kanchipuram,
Tamil Nadu, 8th c. C.E.

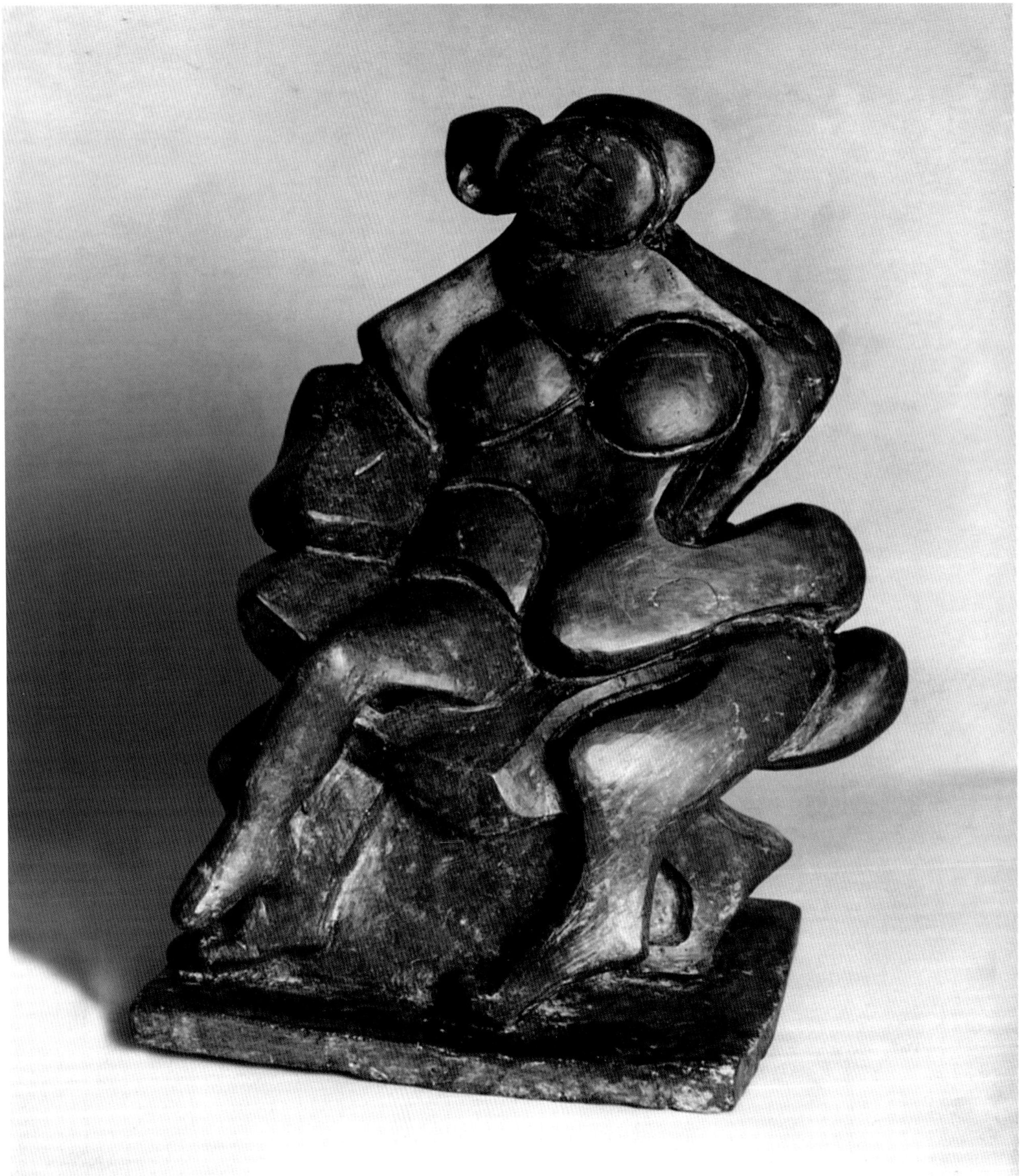

Fig. 23: **Durga on Lion**

Carmel Berkson,
Bronze, 11" x 9" x 18½"

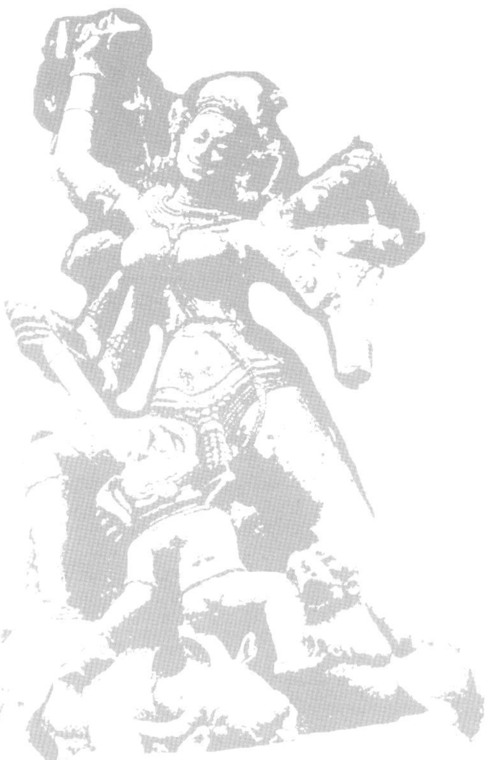

Mahishamardini

Mahishamardini
(Figs. 24-31)

In the history of cults and iconography in India, the goddess, in her form of slaying the buffalo demon, plays a dominating role. Even today, thousands upon thousands of idols abound in every urban centre or village environs.

As the story goes, two royal demon Brahmin brothers practised severe austerities for the purpose of acquiring sons. Rambha was promised a wife of his choice. When a beautiful, dark brown she-buffalo offered affectionate amours, Rambha married her. The buffalo Mahisha was born out of the burning pyre of his buffalo mother who had committed *sati* when her husband was murdered.

Here we have the conflation of many streams of the legend – of deity, royalty, Brahmin, demon and animal which were the characteristics attributed to Mahisha. He too had received a boon after severe penances – he would not be killed by any man. As the father Rambha was soon revived, when Mahisha grew to manhood, father and son conquered first the demon world, then the temporal world and finally, Mahisha and his armies conquered heaven and all the gods.

The gods roamed the earth in misery. To regain control, they created a magnificent goddess out of the various parts of their bodies.

When the demon Mahisha, reigning in heaven, now as a god, heard about the newly formed exquisite creature, the goddess Durga, who was sitting on a hill, he declared his love for her. So, transforming himself into a young heroic human prince, he approached her lovingly. She sent out ambivalent signals, both amorous and threatening, but eventually, love turned into a prolonged battle between Mahisha and the goddess Durga. They fought ferociously and wildly. Eventually, the goddess managed to chop off Mahisha's head. When he died, the world was blessed with peace, prosperity and compassion, and he was soon resurrected to sit at the side of the goddess in Heaven.

Early statues openly depict their symbiosis; later, and until today, during the Kolkata Durga festival, Mahisha's human form is emphasized.

Motifs

1. Demon is hero, human and god
2. Male/female ambivalent relationship
3. Beheading as castration
4. Demon/god is resurrected
5. Mahisha as saviour

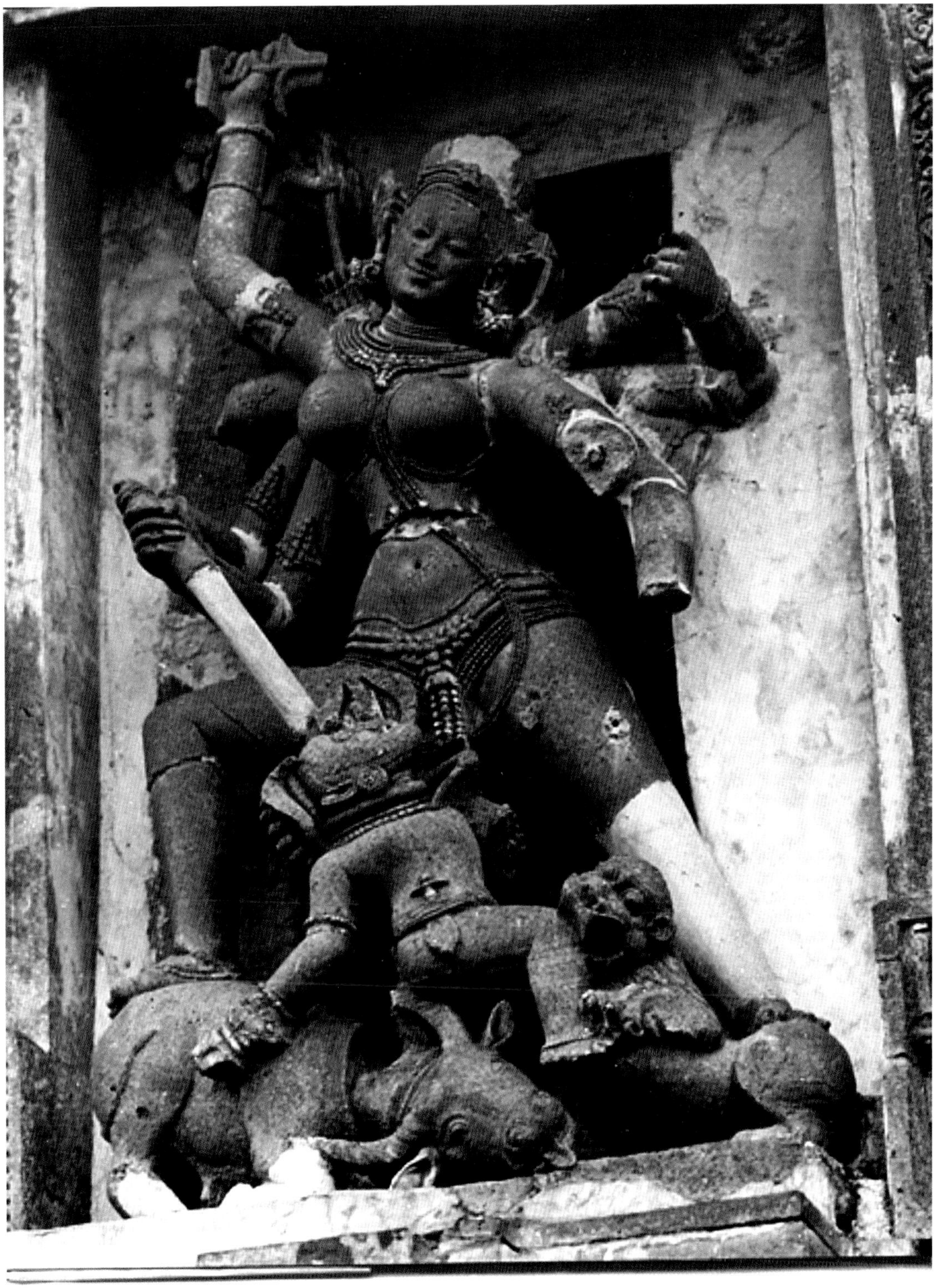

Fig. 24: **Mahishamardini**

Siva Temple,
Khitching,
Orissa, 11th c. C.E.

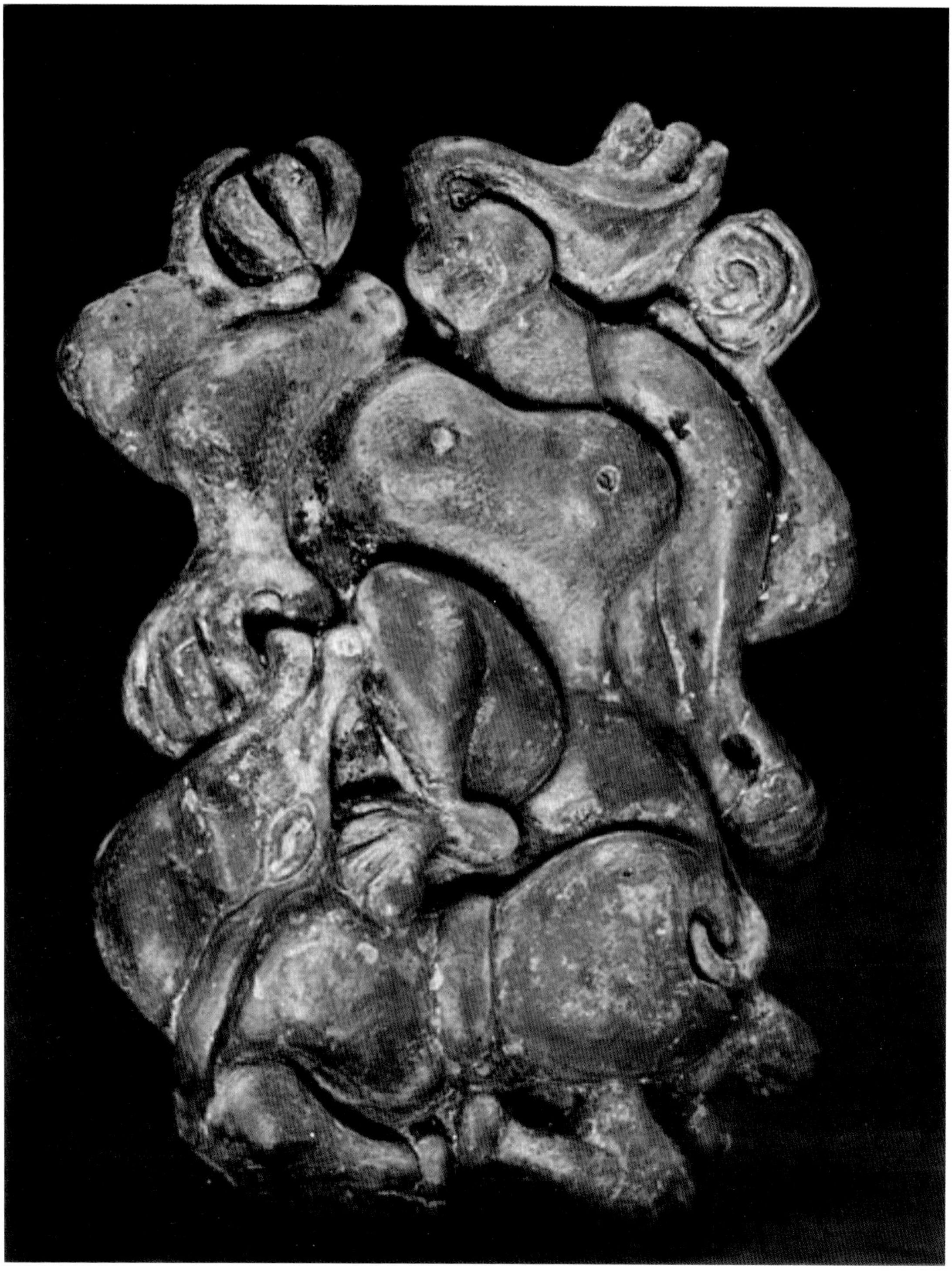

Fig. 25: **Mahishamardini**

Carmel Berkson,
Bronze, Bas relief: 4" x 7"

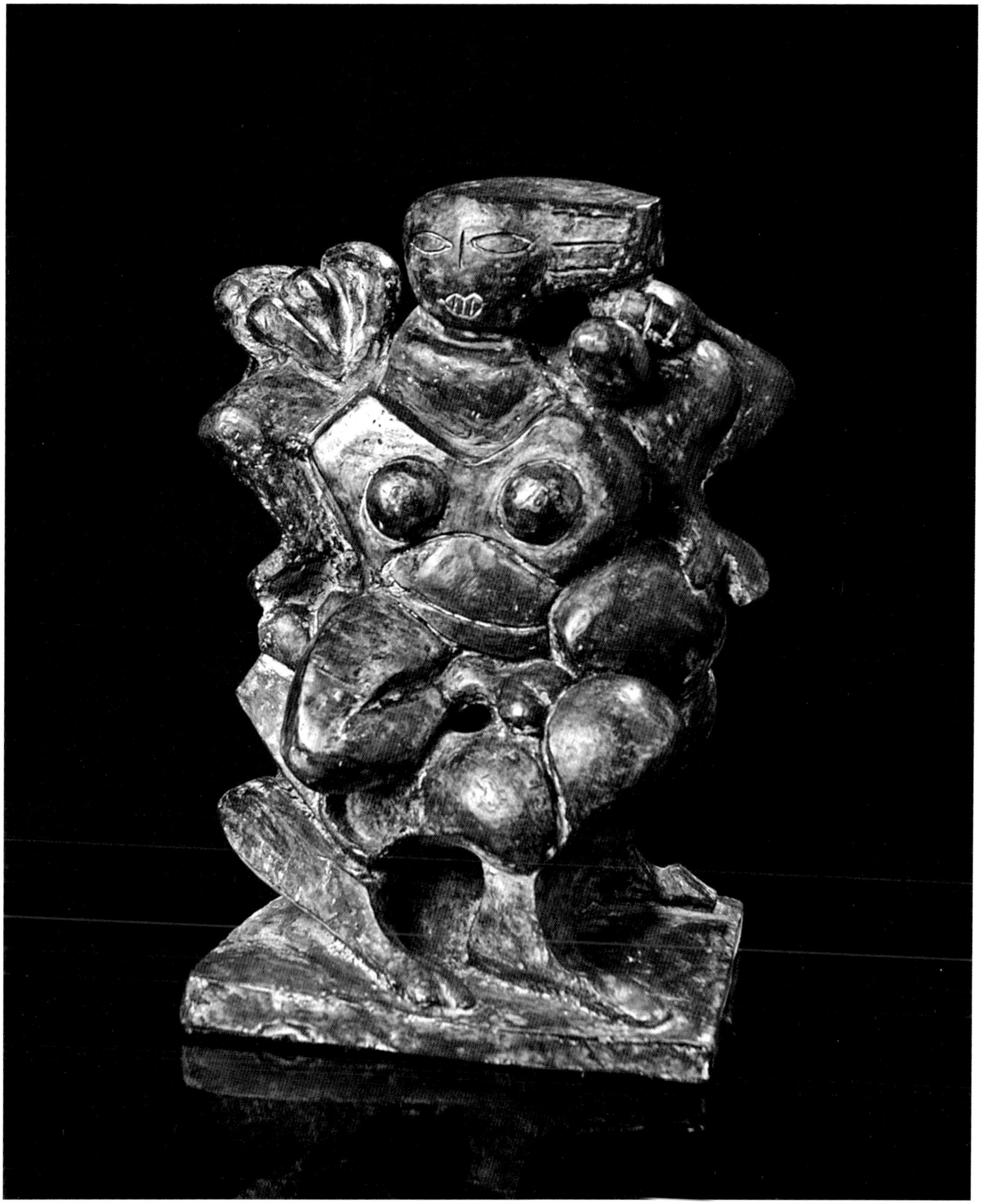

Fig. 26: **Mahishamardini**

Carmel Berkson,
Bronze, 9" x 10½" x 16"

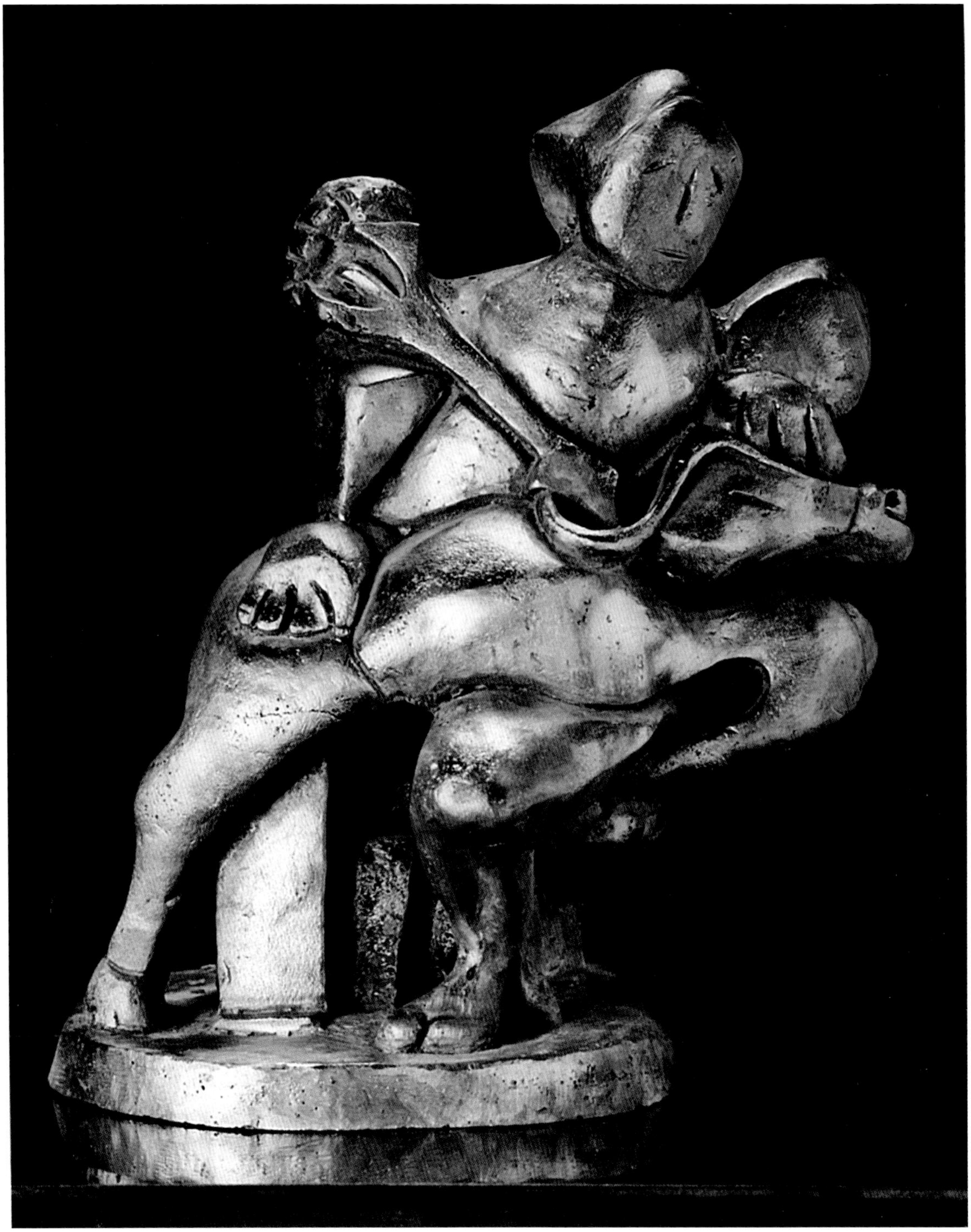

Fig. 27: **Mahishamardini**

Carmel Berkson,
Bronze, 11" x 9" x 16½"

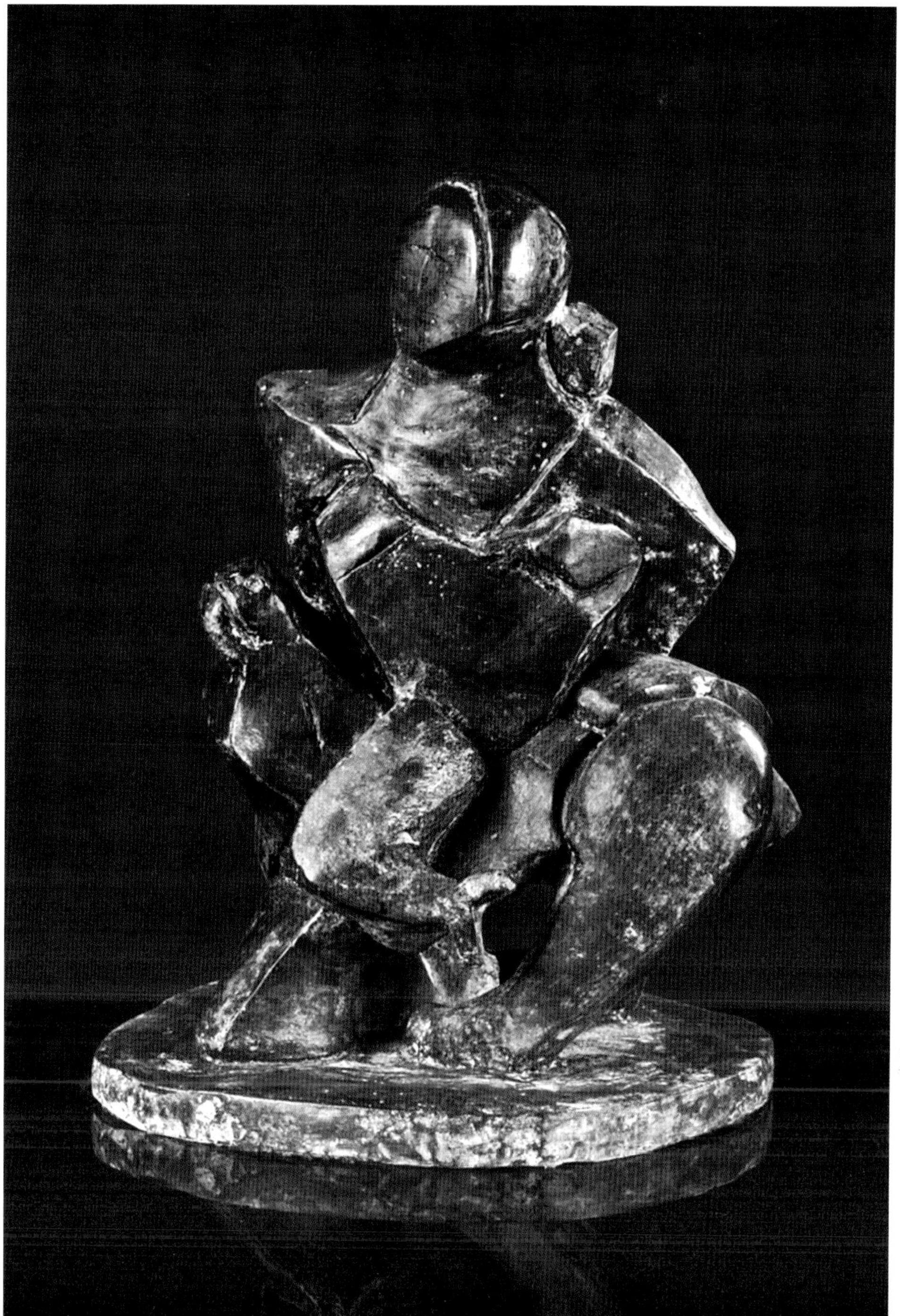

Fig. 28: **Mahishamardini**

Carmel Berkson,
Bronze, 9½" x 9½" x 17"

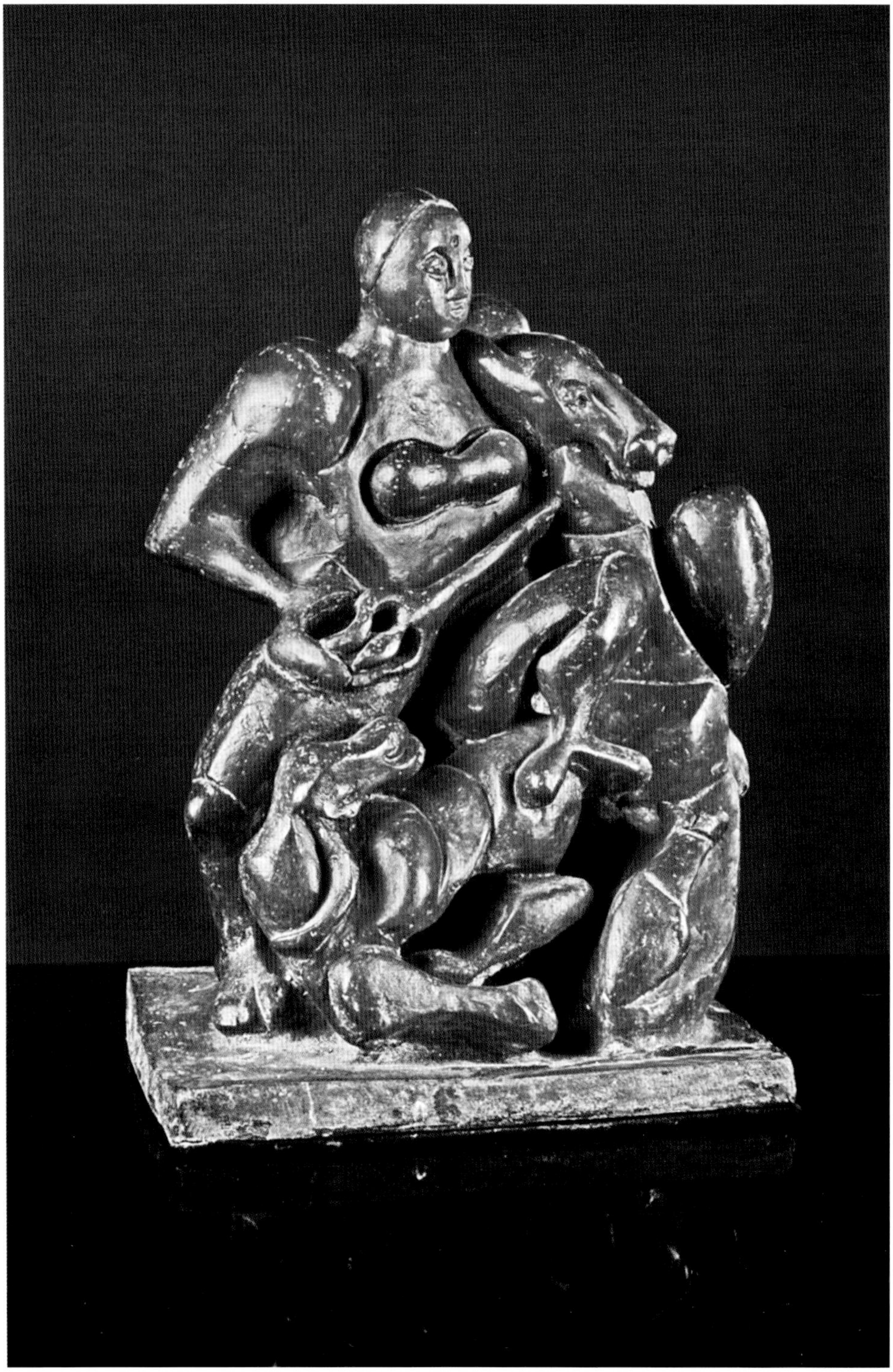

Fig. 29: **Mahishamardini**

Carmel Berkson,
Bronze, 9½" x 8" x 15"

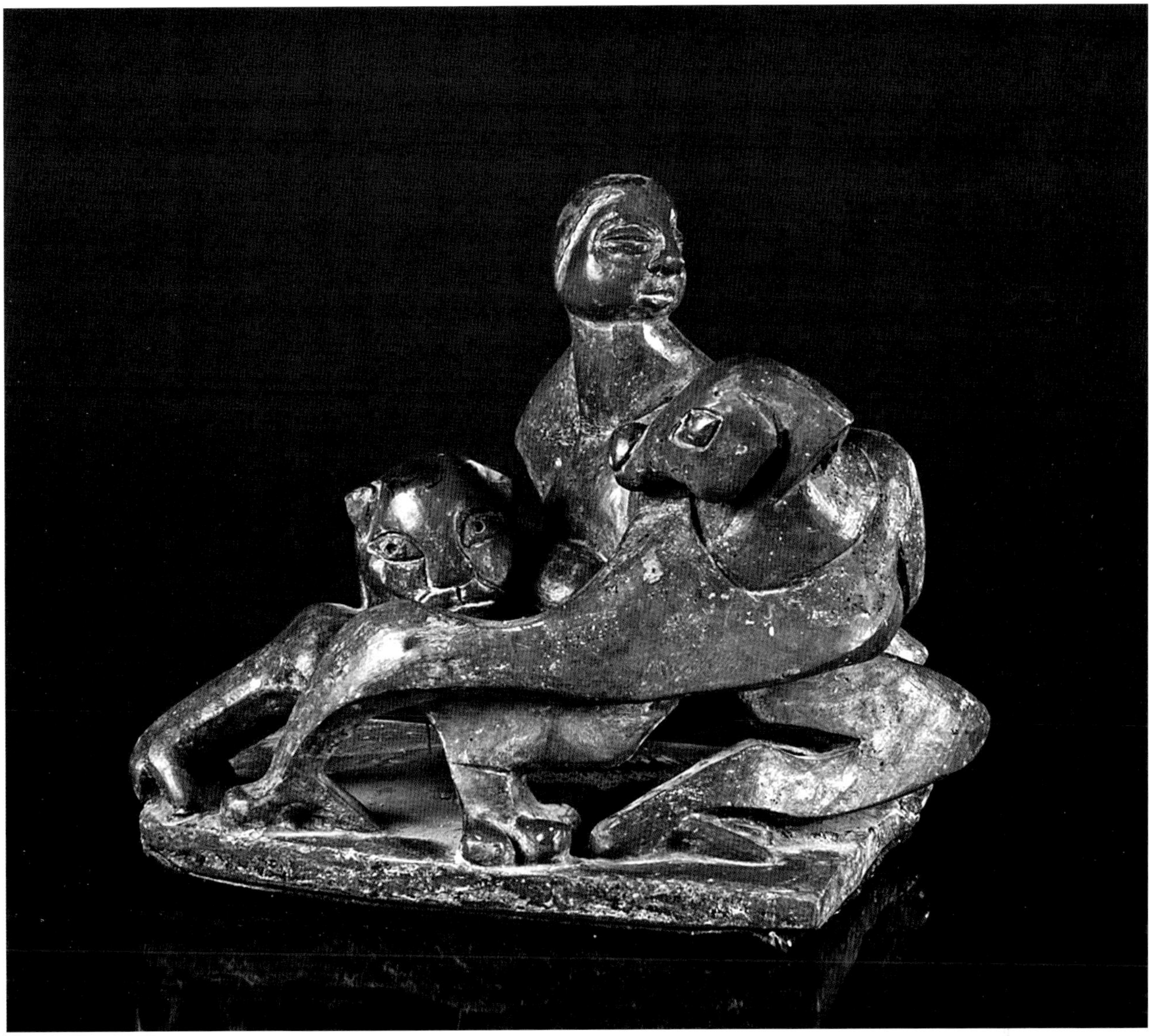

Fig. 30: **Mahishamardini**

Carmel Berkson,
Bronze, 12" x 10" x 14"

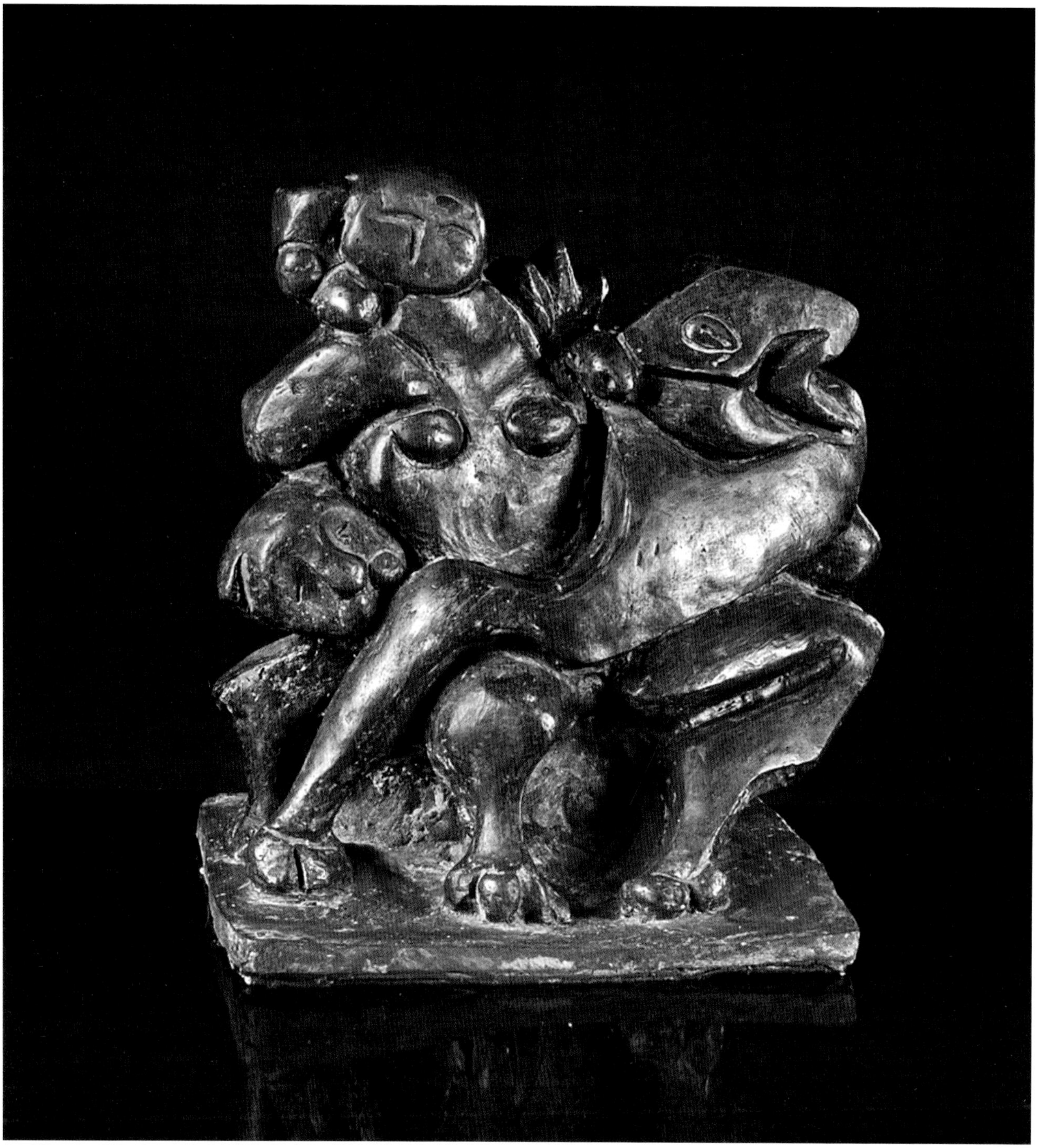

Fig. 31: **Mahishamardini**

Carmel Berkson,
Bronze, 12" x 11" x 15"

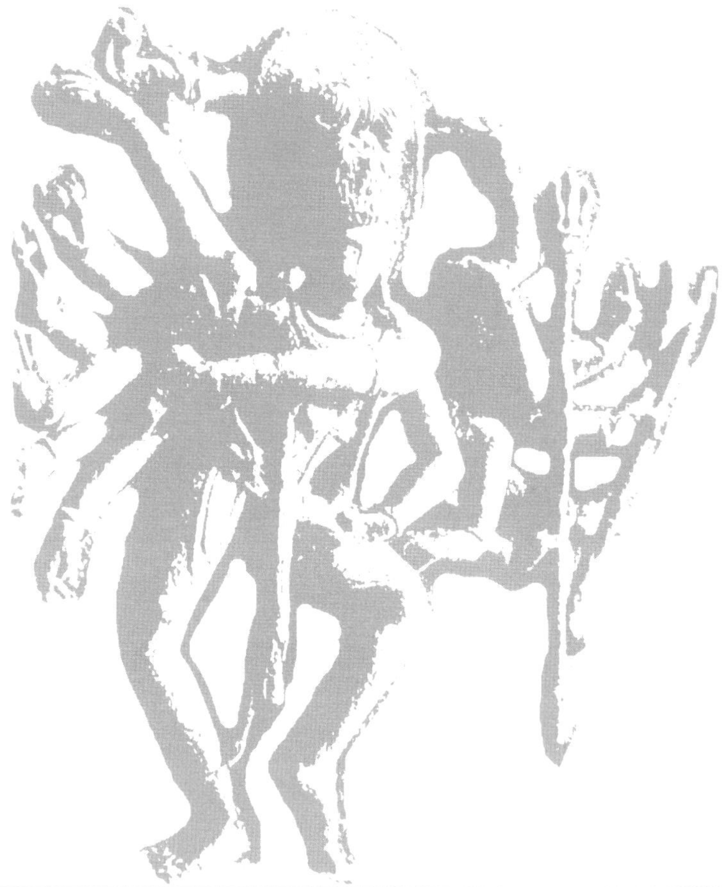

Siva

Nritta Murti – Siva's Dance
(Figs. 32-34)

Siva's dance is the reflection of the eternal, cosmic movements and rhythms. Cosmic time is perpetual, moving in a cyclical pattern of creation, preservation, dissolution and recreation. This is Siva's dance. His activity creates life out of inert nature. "I am the creator, the promulgator of eternal laws, everything is within me and I am everything."

Time, primal energy, movement – all processes of nature are Siva's dance. He dances in the cremation ground at Chidambaram, the navel of the universe. As Siva lifts the veil of *maya*, the devotee comes to realize that the burning ground is the locus of his/her own heart, beating to the rhythms of the entire cosmos, of cyclical time and mobility. The dance heals by destroying the bonds of *karma*, illusion and the individual ego. Release, salvation and grace follows.

Siva dances on Apasamara. The dwarf demon is associated with snakes, disease and/or amnesia and is greatly feared; sometimes he even attacks the gods. They approach Siva as saviour, and he dances on the body of the demon, to the rhythm of the drum beat. While Siva's foot annihilates, simultaneously it releases.

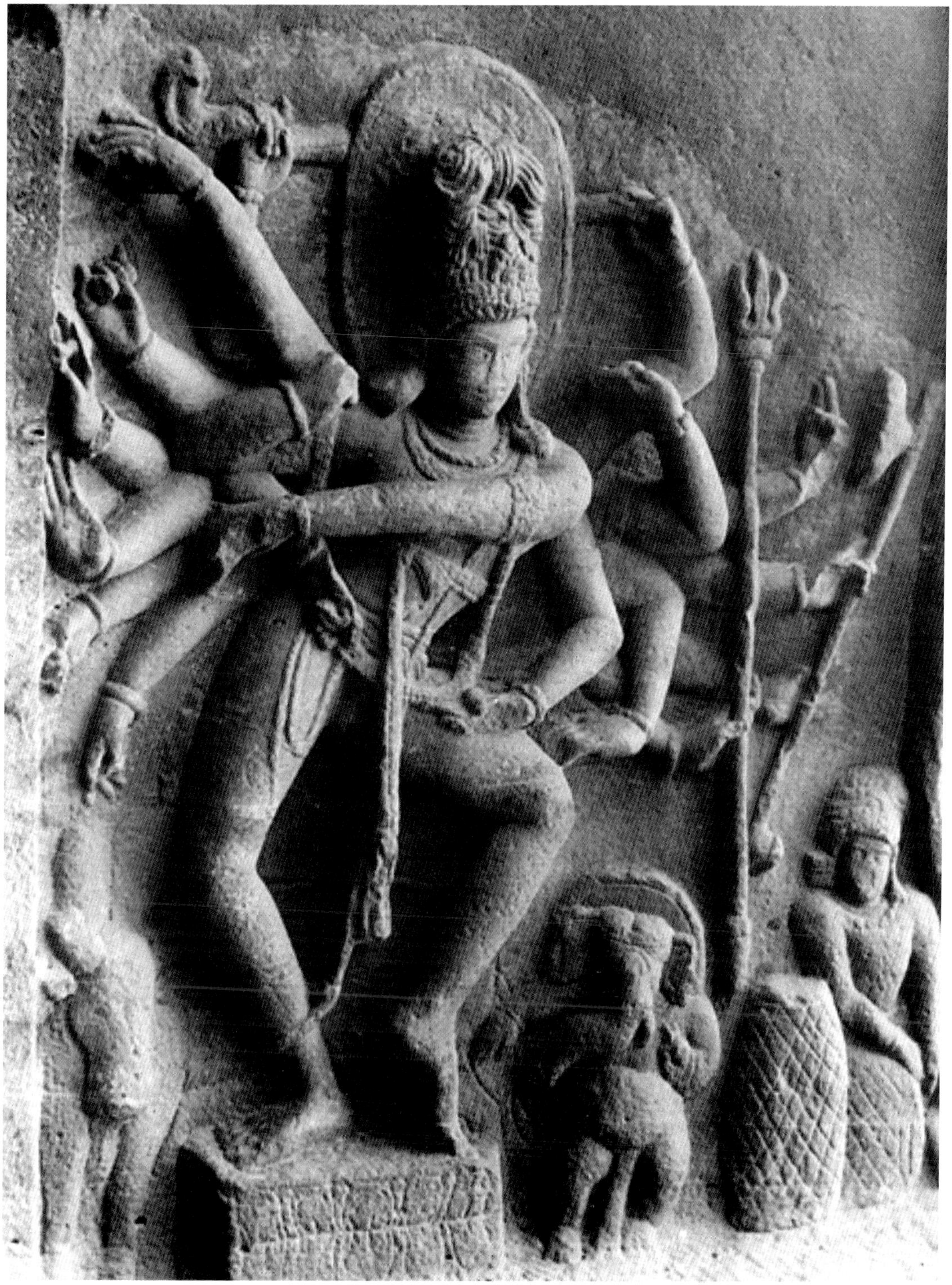

Fig. 32: **Siva Dancing in Lalita, Nritta Murti** Badami, Karnataka, 6th c. C.E.

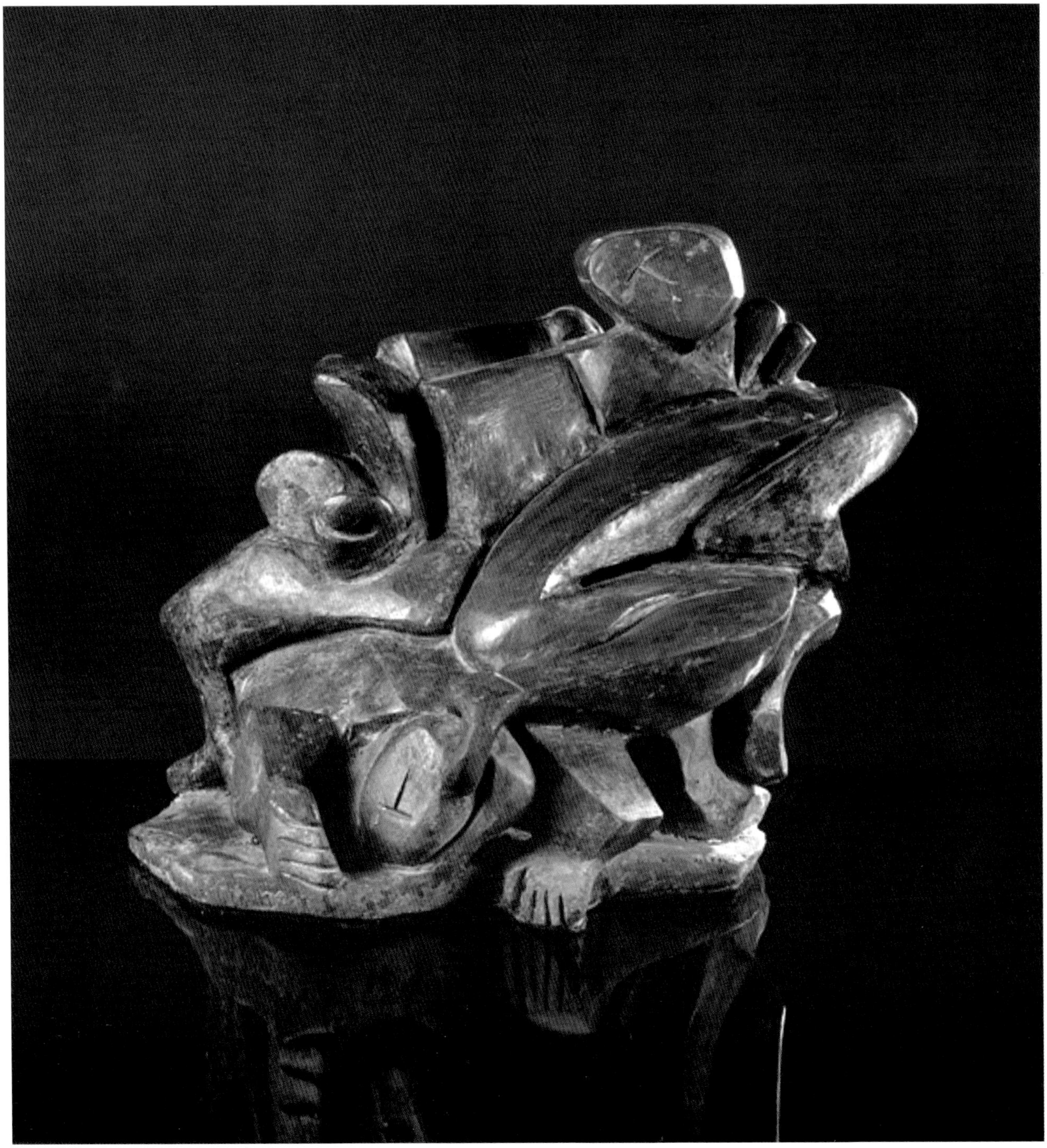

Fig. 33: **Siva Dancing on Apasamara, Nritta Murti**

Carmel Berkson,
Bronze, 13" x 12" x 16"

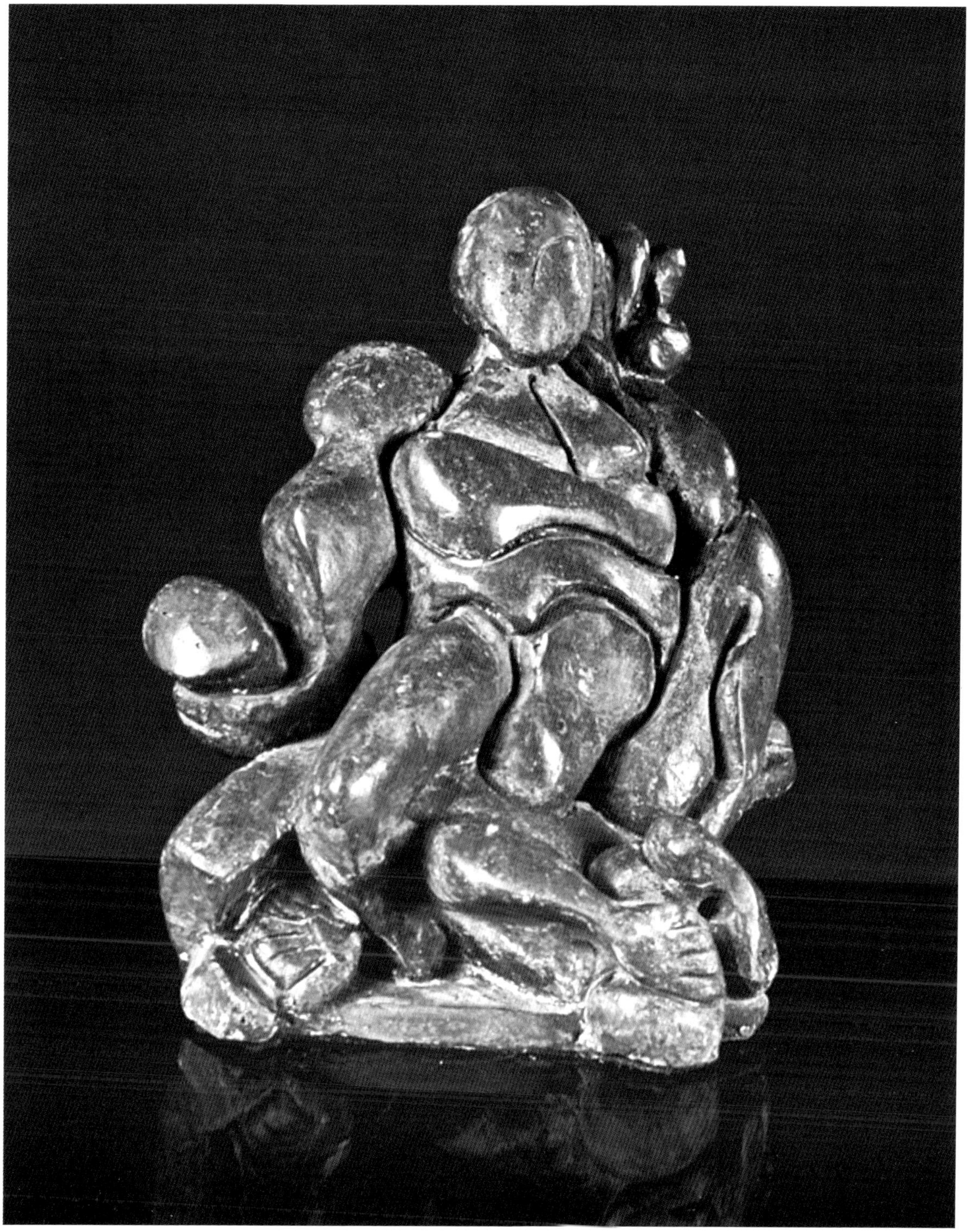

Fig. 34: **Siva Dancing on Apasamara, Nritta Murti**

Carmel Berkson,
Bronze, 8" x 7" x 14"

Siva as Kala – Kala, the Destroyer of Death
(Fig. 35)

As told in the Sangam literature, the poet Markandeyan practised severe austerities for the purpose of acquiring a son. When asked by Siva whether he wished to have a dull son who would live out his years, or one who would be brilliant and pious but would die at age sixteen, the poet chose the latter.

The son Markandeya reached the age of sixteen. As was his habit, he was in the act of worshipping Siva when Yama, the god of death, appeared with the intention of taking the boy. As the noose around his neck was about to be tightened, Siva sprang from the *linga*. He kicked Yama on the chest with his outstretched leg. Thus the god of death died. The boy was saved and was granted immortality.

The Saiva saint Sambandhar sings:

"In sleep and when not sleeping
With melting heart, meditate daily.
It was the five letters which kicked the god of death
And struck him with terror
When he came to take the life of Markandeya
Who, without guile in his heart,
Came to pay obeisance to the feet of the Lord Civan."[1]

Motifs

1. Austerities result in favours from god
2. Siva rewards his devotees
3. Even the god of death dies, but is soon revived
4. Siva tests his devotees

[1]Periyar Puranam.

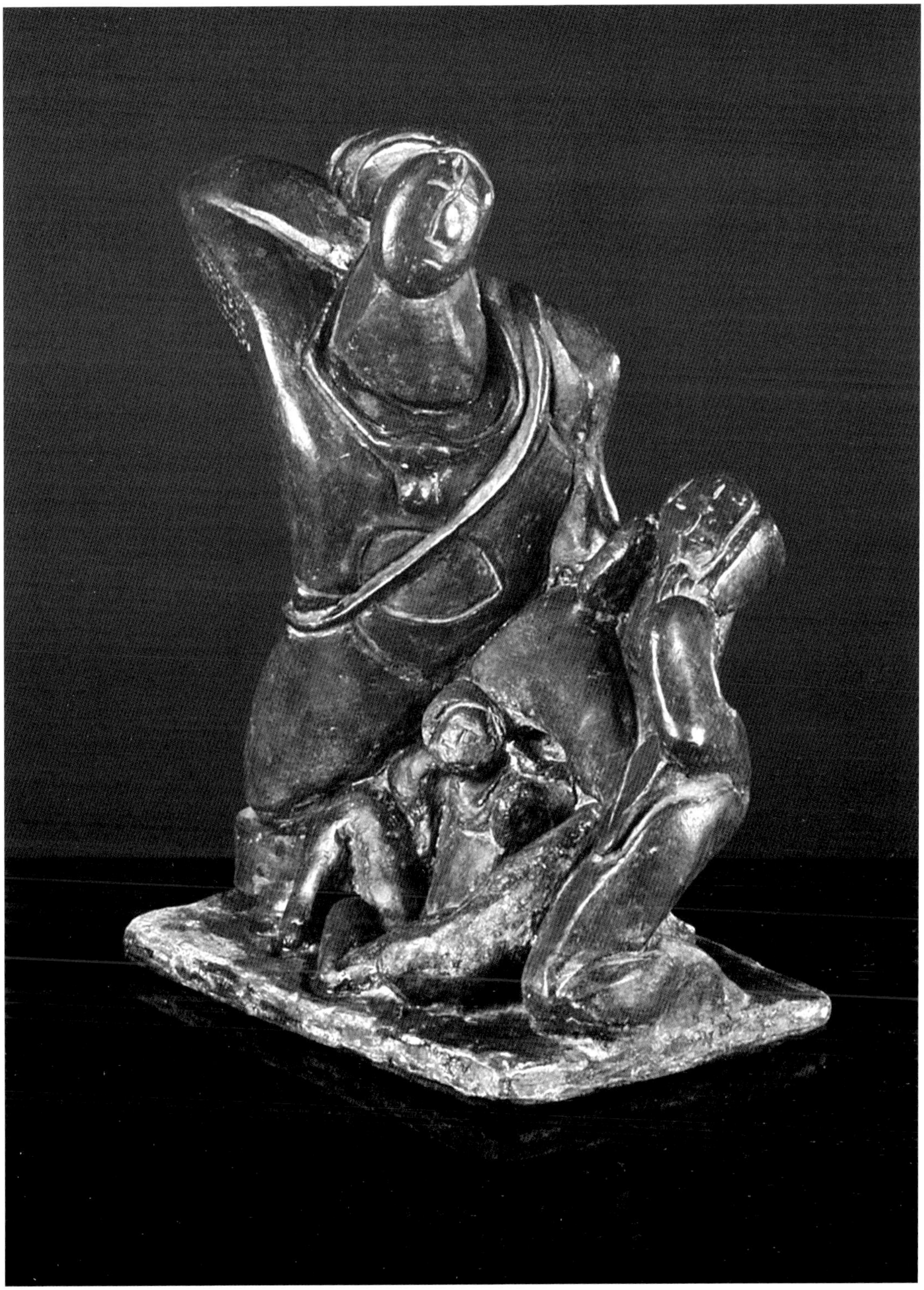

Fig. 35: **Siva as Kala – Kala, the Destroyer of Death**

Carmel Berkson,
Bronze, 10½" x 7½" x 14"

Submarine Fiery Mare – Vadavanala (Fig. 36)

While Siva sat in deep meditation, Kama approached, aiming his arrow at the god. "A great flame of fire sprang from the third eye of the infuriated Siva",[1] reducing the god of love to ashes. So great were the flames, and so rapidly did the fire spread that very soon the entire universe was threatened with extinction.

The frightened gods went to Brahma, begging his intervention. Brahma concentrated the wild conflagration into the form of a fiery mare. He then approached the ocean and firmly persuaded it to contain the fiery mare in its depths. "This fury of Lord Siva, now in the form of a mare, you will bear till the time of dissolution of all living beings."[2]

Blazing with flames, the mare entered the waters. "Thou art the mare's head, raging within the ocean, ceaselessly vomiting fire and drinking the saline waters as if they were sacrificial butter."[3]

But even while the waters sustain the fire, the mare perennially consumes the overabundance of water flowing from the rivers into the seas, controlling the floods. When Siva will return and release the mare, the entire universe will be dissolved by the resultant conflagrations.

Motifs

1. Opposites integrated but separate: ocean/water
2. God as destructive fire
3. Death of love
4. Transformability of matter: horse/fire

---

[1]Siva Purana, Rudrasamhita, 19:14.

[2]Ibid., 20:17.

[3]Mhb., 13.17.54.

Thanks to Wendy Doniger.

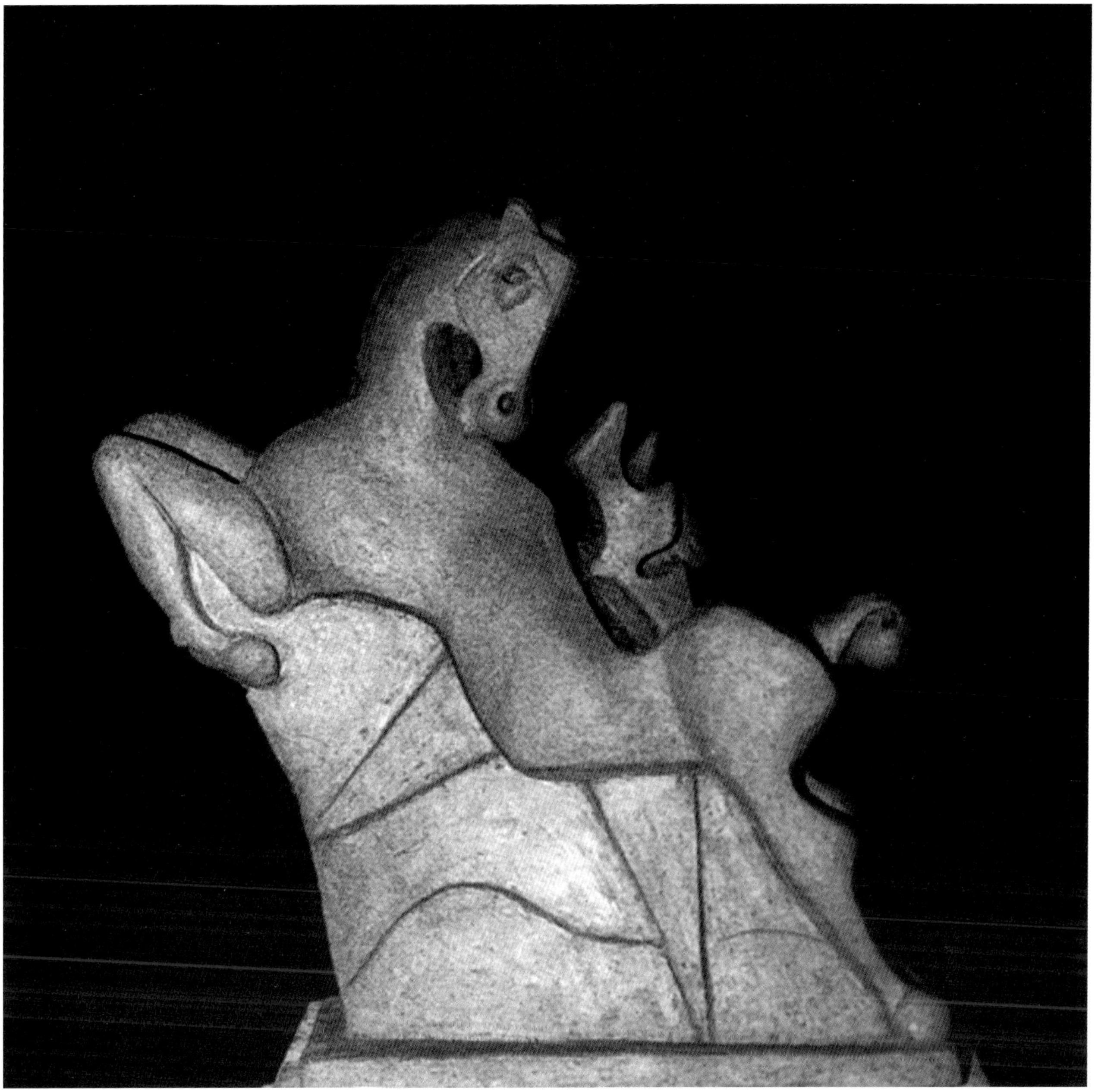

Fig. 36: **Submarine mare, Vadavanala**

Carmel Berkson,
Bronze, 14" x 7" x 19"

Andhakasura
(Figs. 37-38)

The Puranas explain Andhakasura's filial relation to Siva. In a former birth, the demon Hiranyaksa, having pleased Siva by prolonged worship and ascetic exercise, extracted a boon of acquiring a son.

At another time, as Siva sat in deep meditation, standing behind him, Parvati playfully covered his three eyes. Immediately darkness descended on the entire universe. The "rapturous rutting juice exuded from her hands became hot by the fire of Siva's eye and flowed out in copious drops."[1] As she was thus in contact with Siva, a son was born. But because Hiranyaksa had committed so many sins in the past, and the universe was in darkness, the son Andhaka was born malformed and blind. Nevertheless, Siva and Parvati claimed him as their own son.

When he grew to manhood, Andhaka also performed austerities. Brahma offered boons, and thereby the demon became very powerful, conquering earth and heaven, enjoying all the prerogatives of the gods. He was full with pride, arrogant and heedful of nothing outside himself.

He once saw his mother, Parvati, meditating in a cave on Mt. Mandara. Entirely deluded, he lusted after her. "He wished to snatch her from the Lord."[2] Even though his ministers reminded him over and over again that his intentions were sinful, since Parvati was in actuality his mother, Andhaka persisted in his passion. "He would be my friend, my ally, my brother, my father, who may bring to me that daughter of the mountain."[3]

Andhaka spoke rudely to the meditating Siva, ordering the god to surrender the young and beautiful lady. The wildly angered Siva, with Viraha and thousands upon thousands of *ganas*, entered into a prolonged battle with the armies of the blind demon son. But the battle was very vicious, for, when the drops of blood from Andhaka's wounds fell to the ground, new Andhakas with hideous faces were born. Finally Andhaka – and all the Andhakas – was killed. Staked to Siva's trident he was held aloft in the sky, dried up by the rays of the sun and drenched with gusts of wind and heavy downpours. Andhaka remained there for thousands of years. Eventually, he was redeemed and became a devotee of Siva and again Siva and Parvati claimed him as their son.

Motifs

1. Sins of the father inflicted on the son
2. Incestual longing
3. Attempted filicide
4. Blood as creative
5. Redemption through sacrifice in battle
6. Father/son reconciliation

---

[1]Siva Purana, Rudrasamhita, 42, 18.

[2]Matsya Purana, Vol. II, 179, 2, 7.

[3]Vamana Purana, 37, 3.

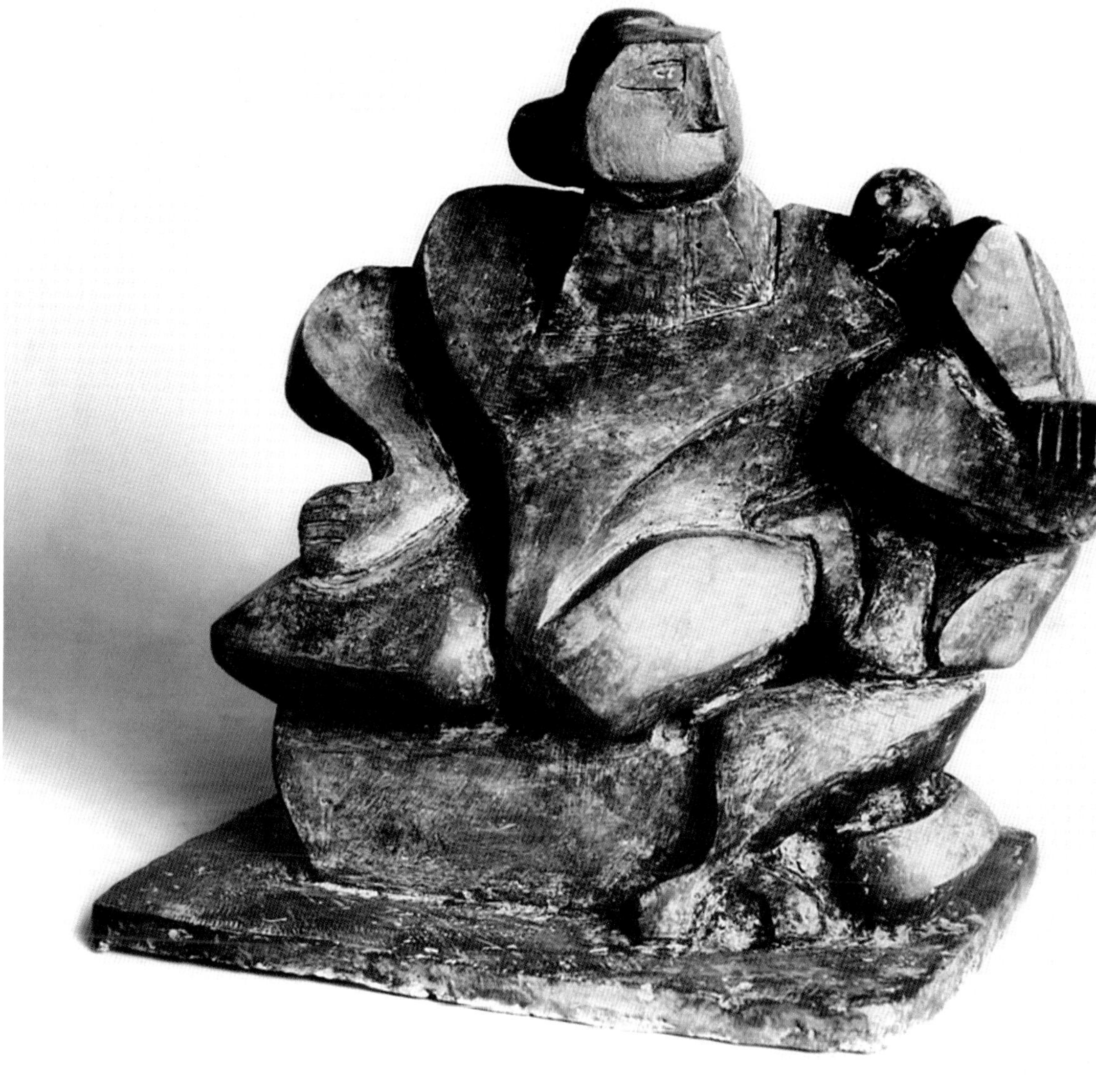

Fig. 37: **Andhakasura**

Carmel Berkson,
Bronze, 12" x 8½" x 14"

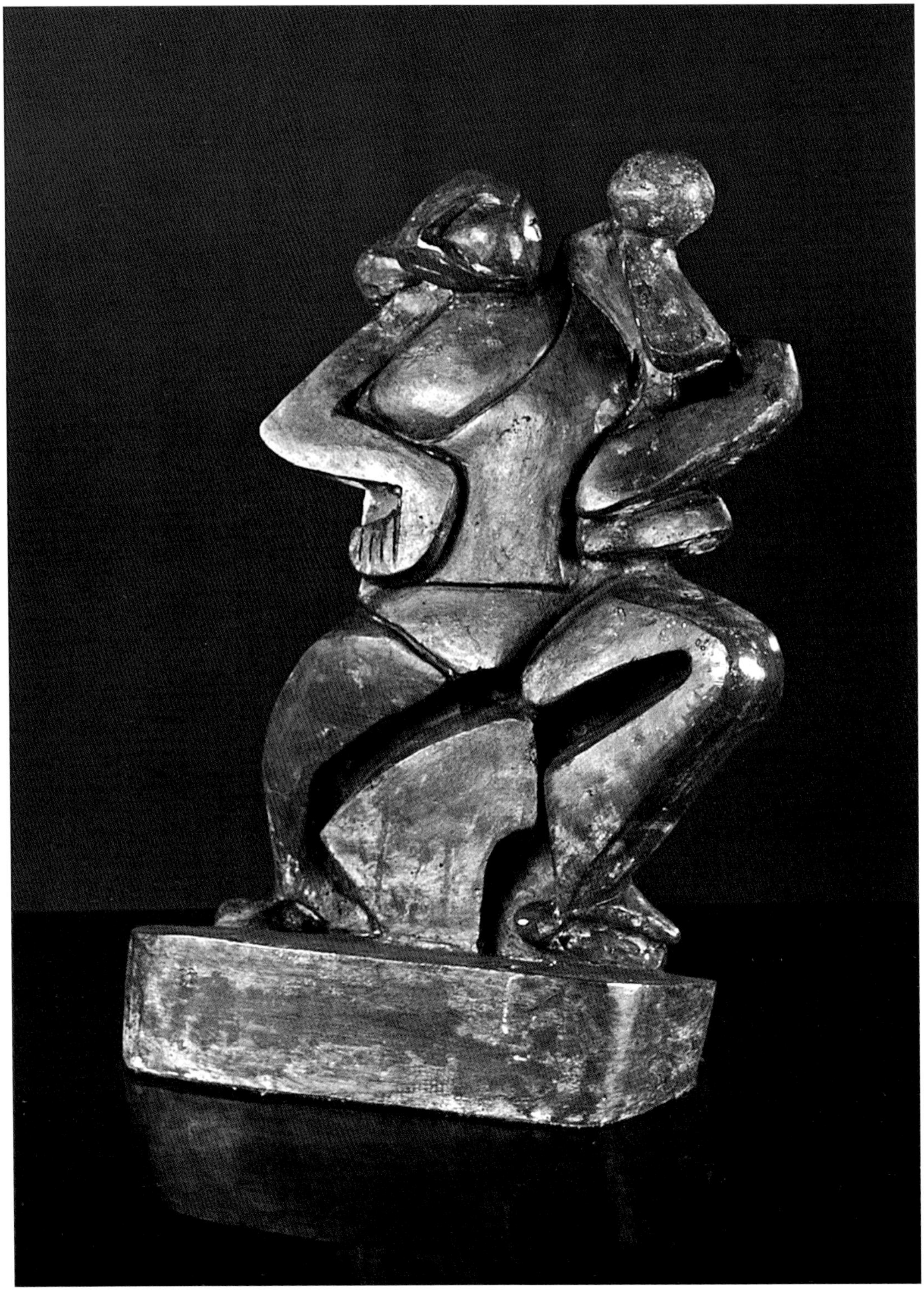

Fig. 38: **Andhakasura**

Carmel Berkson,
Bronze, 13" x 7" x 16"

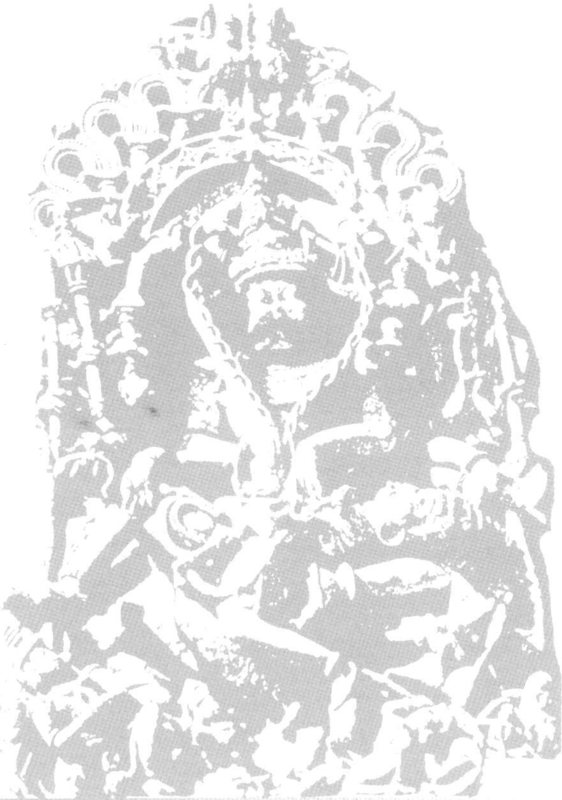

Visnu-Krishna

Narasimha/ Hiranyakasipu (Figs. 39-40)

Hiranyakasipu received an extraordinary boon from Brahma who was happy with the demon's rigorous austerities: "May I not die at the hands of anything created, at daytime or at night, indoors or outdoors, on land or in the sky and by any weapon whatsoever. May I also be lord of all beings and have my powers of penance intact."[1]

As a consequence, Hiranyakasipu conquered the earth, oceans, mountains and eventually heaven too. He was wicked and oppressed the people. He even ordered the execution of his own son, a worshipper of Visnu. "Overwhelmed with unbearable (violent) wrath, and with eyes reddened with anger Hiranyakasipu ordered: ...this boy deserves capital punishment. Let him be executed immediately."[2]

The son Prahlada persisted in his worship, claiming that Visnu is everywhere. His father retorted: "As you are vaunting too much, I now sever your head from the trunk. Let Hari, who you trust as protector, save you."[3] At that moment, Hiranyakasipu sprang from his throne, knocked a pillar which was not inside nor outside with his fist. It was twilight. Amidst a terrific crash of pillars, Visnu manifested as man-lion. "The body was terrible and refulgent, like a crore of suns, blazing and powerful like the fire at the time of dissolution."[4] A battle ensued and finally Hiranyakasipu was gored by the claws of the lion. Heaven was regained by the gods.

Motifs

1. Powers gained by austerities
2. Transformations: god/animal
3. Filicide threat

[1-4]Srimad Bhagavatam, BK VIII, Chap. 104.

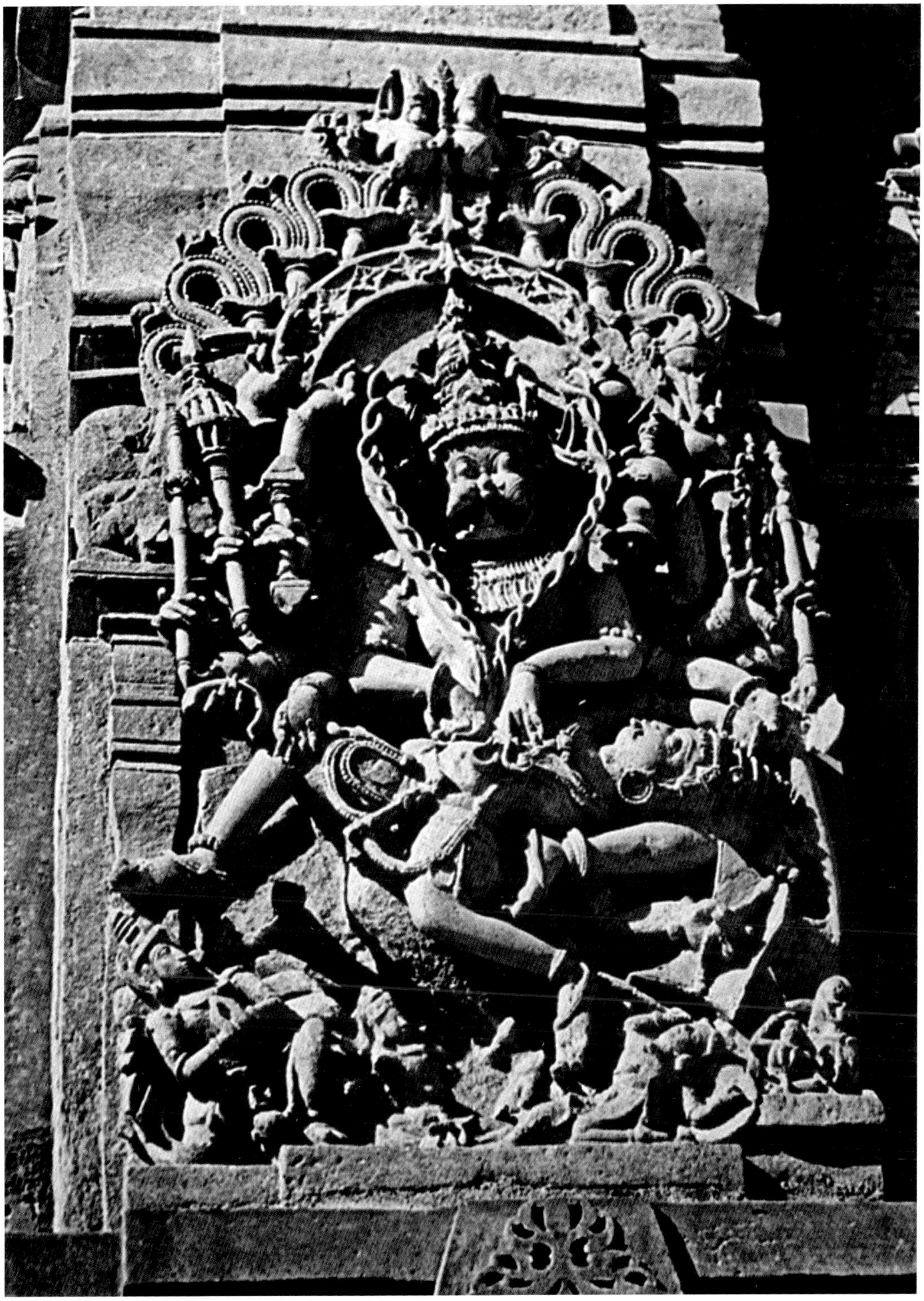

Fig. 39: **Narasimha/Hiranyakasipu**

Hoysalesvara Temple,
Halebid,
Karnataka, 11th c. C.E.

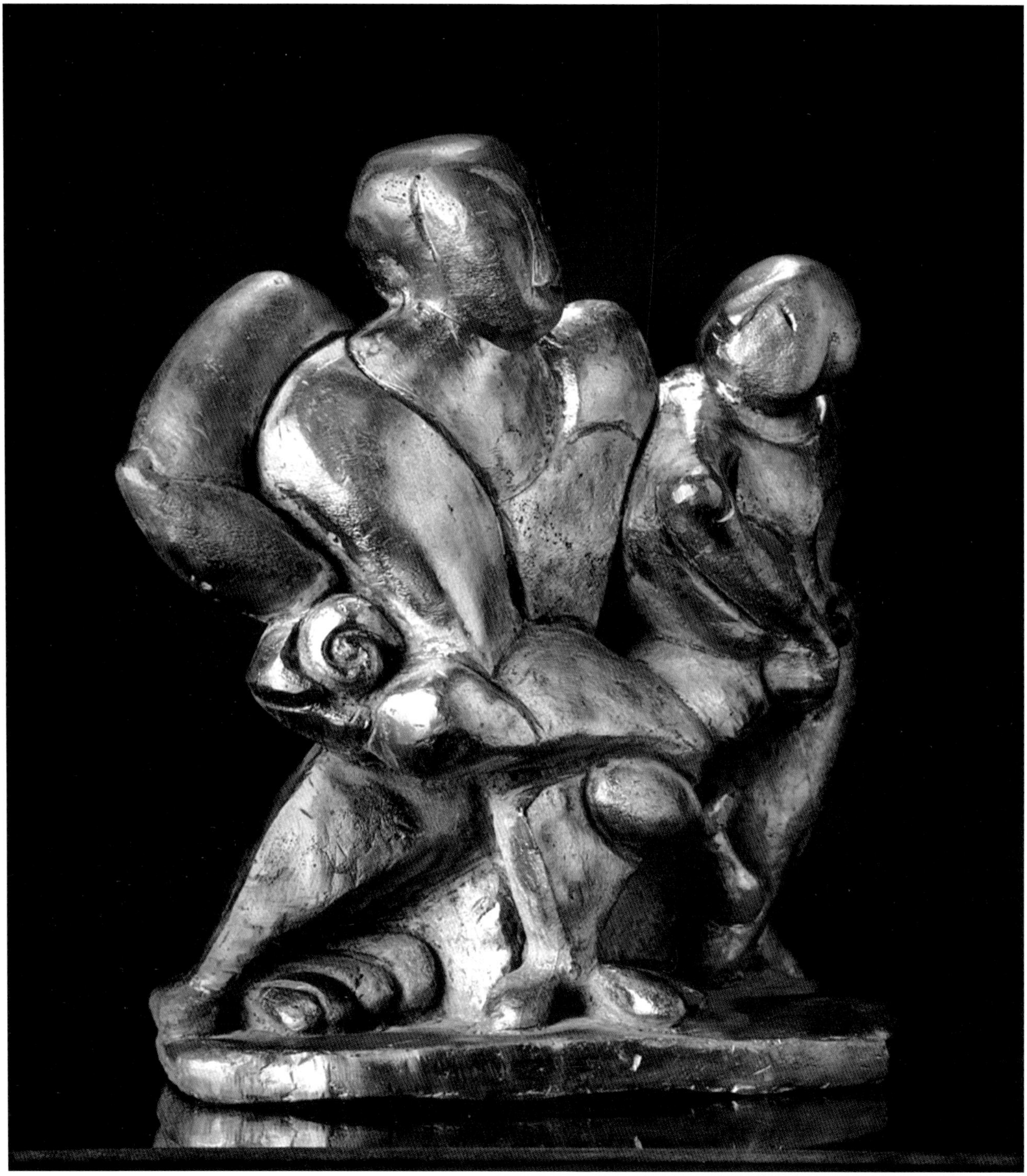

Fig. 40: **Pattern, structure, system**

Narasimha/Hiranyakasipu
Carmel Berkson,
Bronze, 12" x 7" x 15"

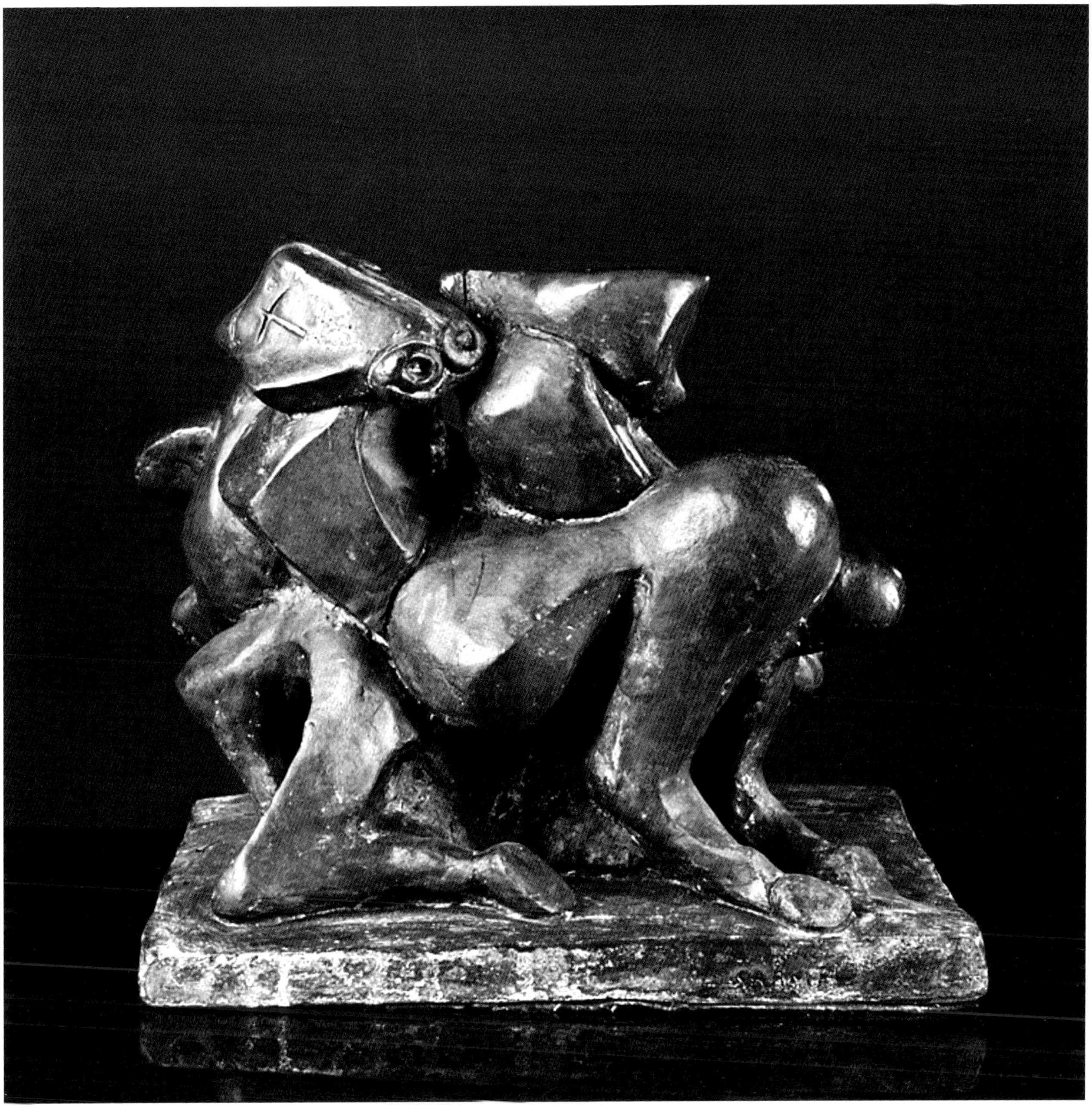

Fig. 41: **Laksmi and Visnu as mare and horse** Carmel Berkson, Bronze, 14" x 11" x 12"

Laksmi and Visnu as Mare and Horse (Figs. 41-42)

As Revanta, the son of the Sun, came riding on his beautiful horse on his way to see Visnu, "the goddess Laksmi became very much astonished and steadily gazed at him."[1]

When Visnu asked her who was coming, Laksmi did not reply. Visnu became jealous and angry, saying: "While sitting before me, you are enchanted with the sight of a horse, then you be born as mare. When you will get a son in the world like me, you will no doubt come again to be my companion."[2]

Though Laksmi pleaded for a return to her former state, Visnu did not respond. She meditated on Siva, who was pleased. He in turn transformed Visnu into a horse. So the god and goddess copulated in the form of horse and mare, and from this union a beautiful horse, Kavira, was born, and Laksmi was restored to her rightful place as the wife of the restored Visnu.

Motifs

1. Jealous god
2. Transfomation of god/goddess/animal

[1-2]Devi Bhagavata Purana, Chap. XVIII.

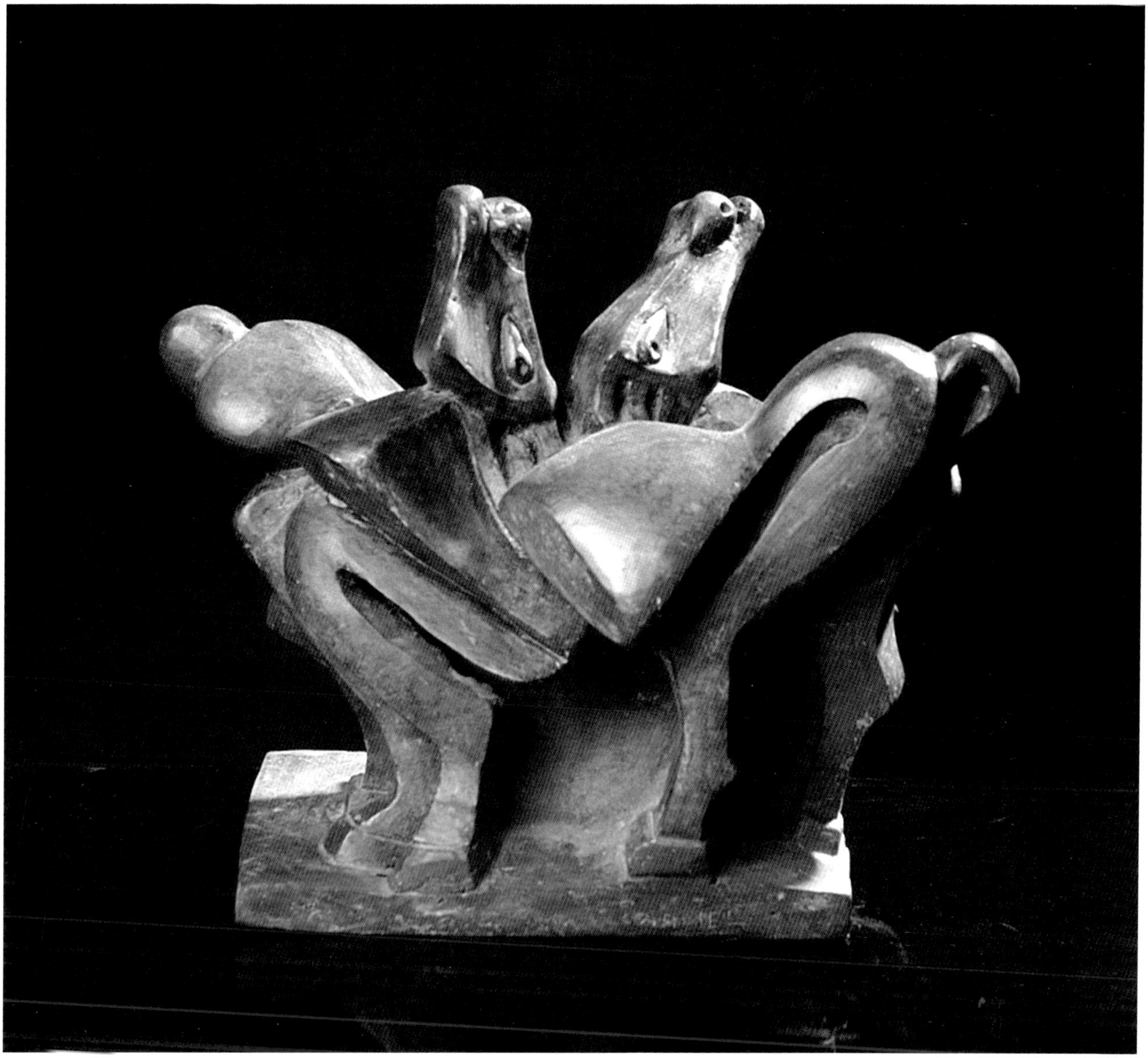

Fig. 42: **Laksmi and Visnu as mare and horse**

Carmel Berkson,
Bronze, 10½" x 8½" x 14"

Gajendramoksha
(Figs. 43, 44, 45)

In a previous birth, King Indradyumna had been a devotee of Visnu, but because of a supposed slight to the *rishi* Agastya, he was cursed to become Gajendra, lord of elephants, who roamed the hills of Trikuta. One day, feeling thirsty, he entered a lake within which a former *gandharva*, Huhu by name, who himself had been cursed by another *rishi* to become a crocodile, awaited. He then "dragged him (Gajendra) with powerful force"[1] and would not let him go. The elephant and the crocodile struggled fiercely in the waters for a thousand years, until finally the former king lost all energy. Then he remembered his former relationship with Visnu and cried out:

> "I've lost my strength/my courage. I'm dying. My body is dead tired; you're my only hope. Save me. Come, lord, help me now."
>
> "Now Visnu, flooded with compassion, cut the crocodile to pieces with the discus that shook the world, sending off sparks that dimmed the sun."[2]

The elephant was soon transformed back into a human, in the image of Visnu, and the *gandharva* was returned to his rightful place.

Motifs

1. Transformability of species
2. Power of austerities
3. Deity's miraculous powers

[1]Bhagavata Purana, VIII, 2, 28.

[2]Thanks to V.N. Rao and David Shulman.

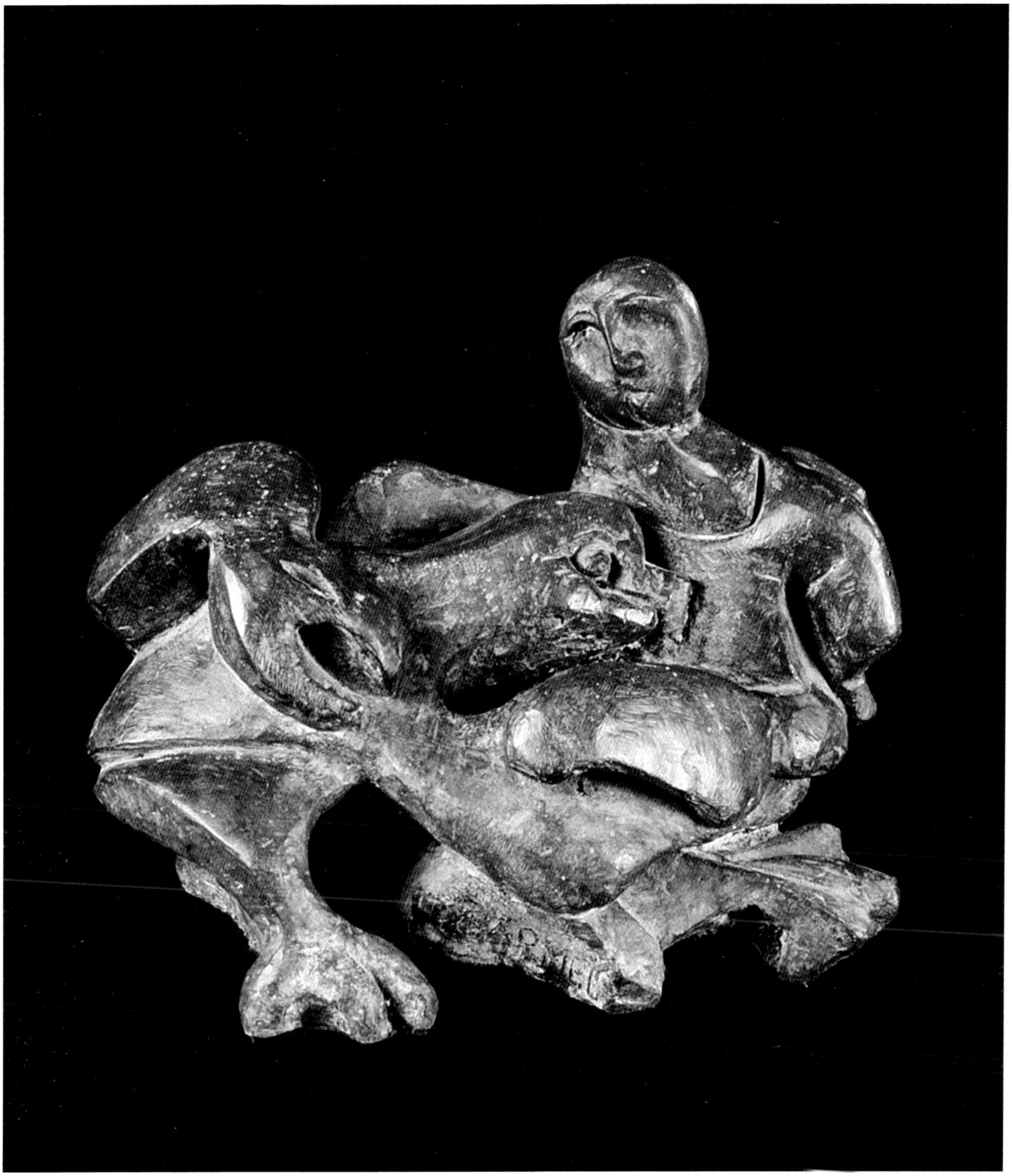

Fig. 43: **Gajendramoksha**

Carmel Berkson,
Bronze, 12" x 9" x 9"

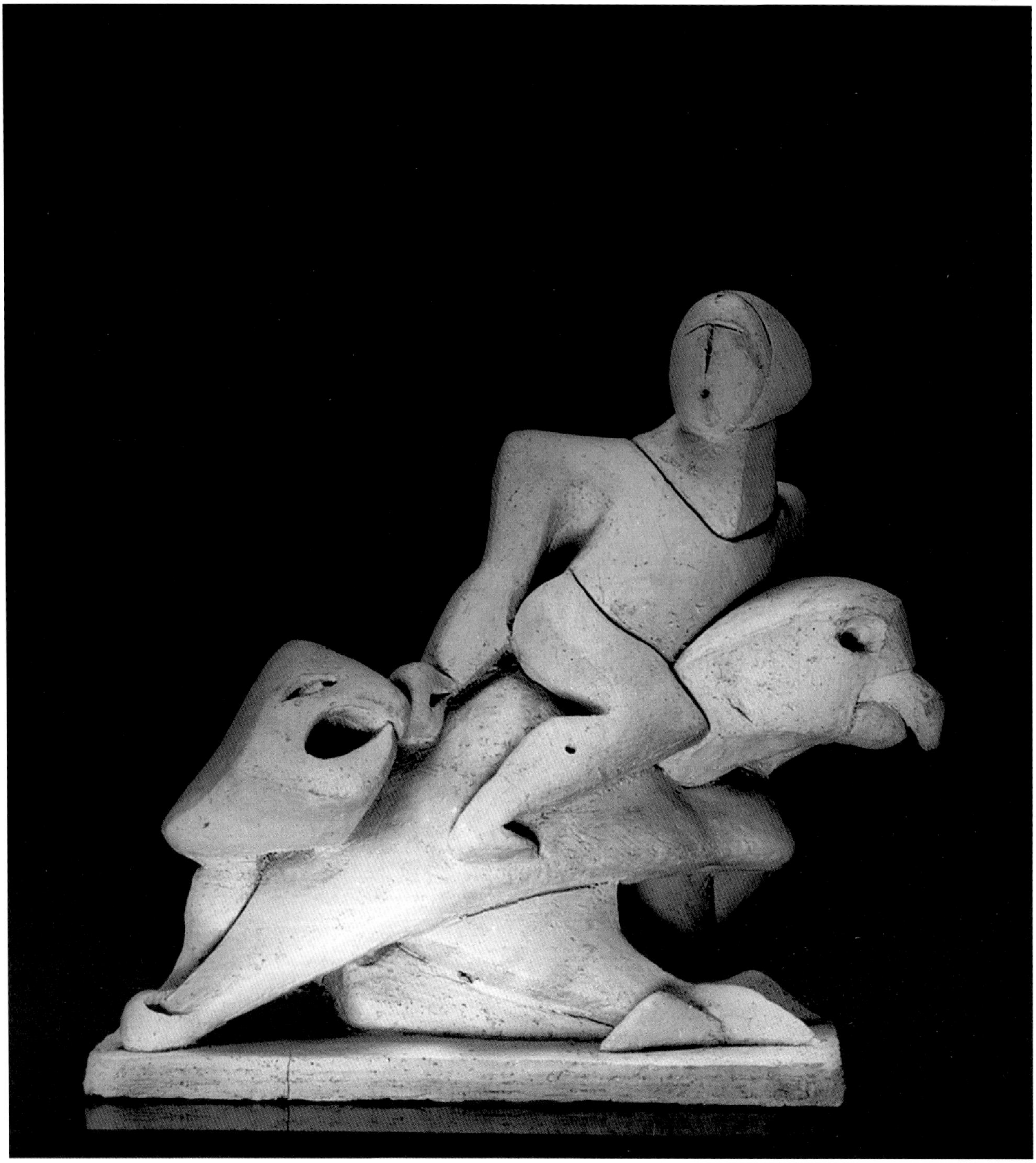

Fig. 44: **Gajendramoksha**

Carmel Berkson,
Bronze, 12" x 10" x 16"

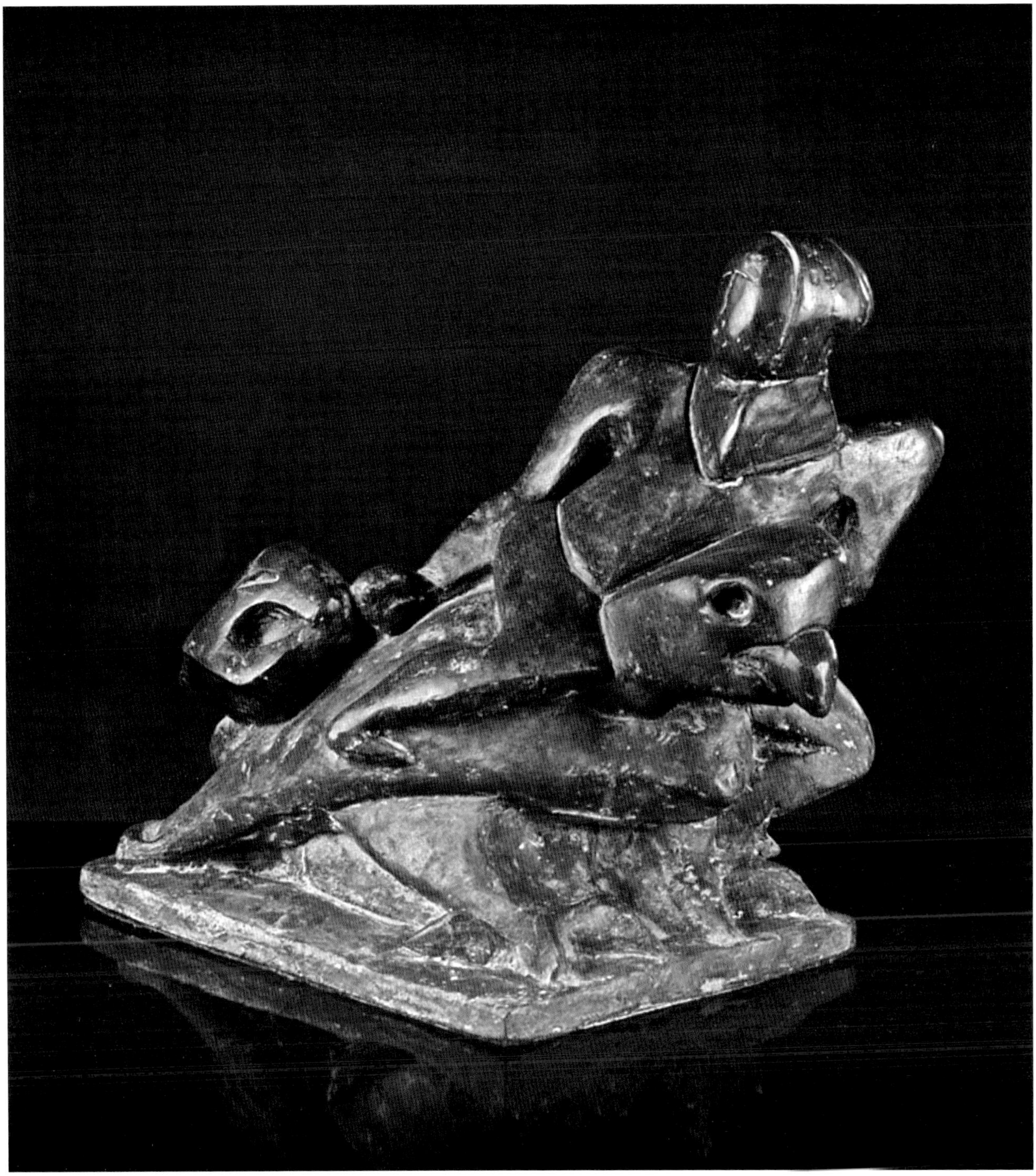

Fig. 45: **Gajendramoksha**

Carmel Berkson,
Bronze, 12" x 10" x 16"

Yajnavaraha
(Fig. 46)

The demon Hiranyaksa vanquished the gods. He bound the earth and carried her down to the nether regions in the primeval waters at the time of *pralaya*, when nothing existed – all was gloom with no air. Visnu slumbered in a nocturnal sleep for a thousand *yugas*.

But then Visnu awoke for the purpose of creation. He knew the earth had been stolen and had been carried into the deep by Hiranyaksa. Visnu transformed himself into a radiant, white boar. Having killed the demon, "this self-supported supporter of the earth, then, with the object of elevating the earth, entered the nether region and raised the earth with his tusk."[1] The earth was then fixed into a stabile condition, so that creation might proceed.

Motifs

1. Demons become gods by means of conquest
2. Overburdened earth undergoes transformation in water
3. God is self-transformed
4. Male/female ambivalent relations

[1]Kurma Purana, 6:9.

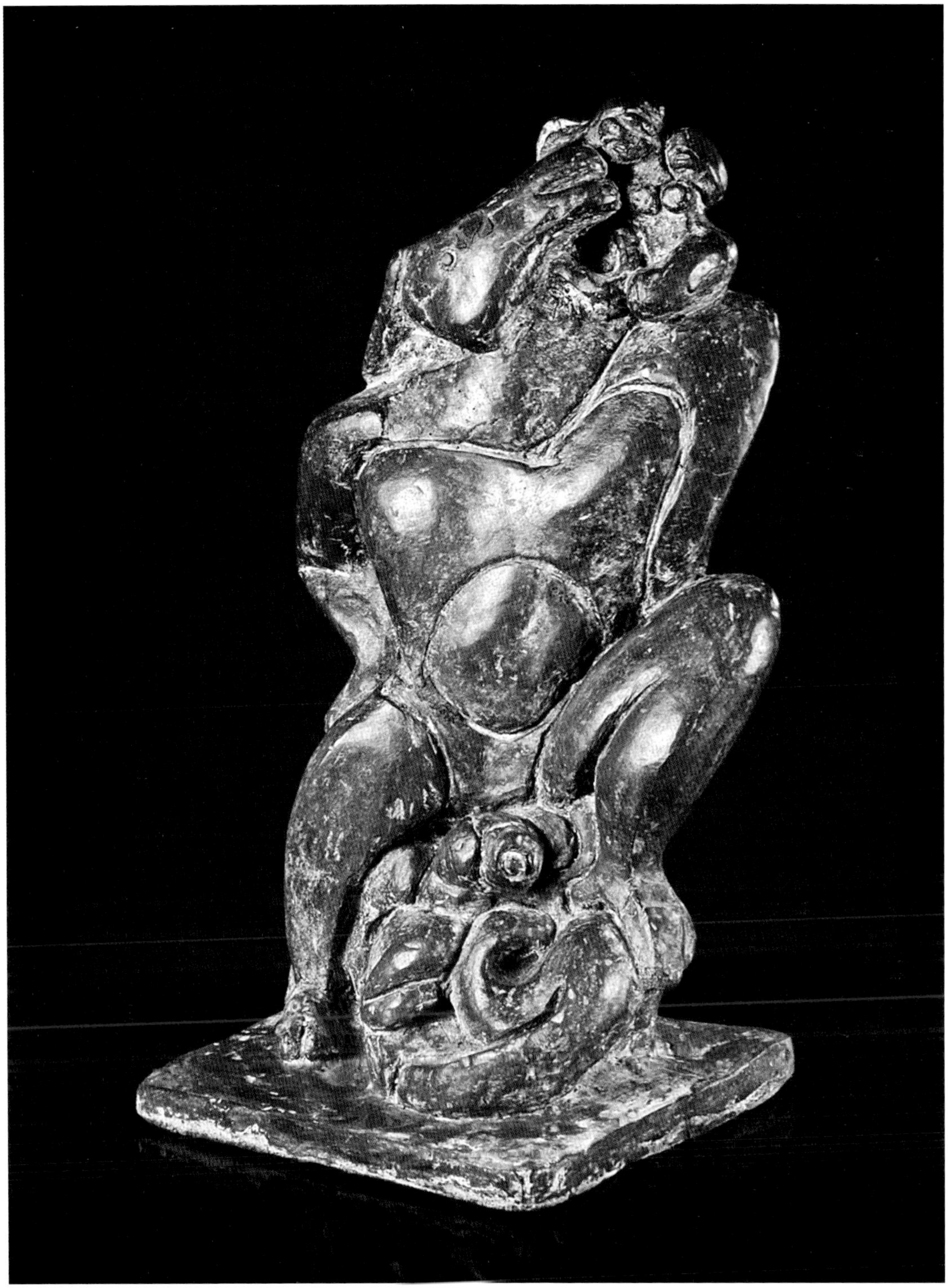

Fig. 46: **Yajnavaraha**

Carmel Berkson,
Bronze, 8½" x 8" x 18"

Garuda battles Serpent (Naga) (Figs. 47-48)

After cosmic separation there is sometimes danger if heaven and earth reconnect. This is symbolized by the battle of the solar bird, the golden feathered eagle, Garuda, with his hereditary enemies – the chthonic snakes. The relationship is a pervasive belief in India and beyond to the East.

Added to this symbolism is the fact that Garuda and the serpents share the same father. Kasyapa had two wives: the first was Kadru, the mother of serpents, while Vinata, the second, was the mother of Garuda. Kadru enslaved Vinata and demanded ambrosia as a condition of her release. Garuda stole ambrosia from the gods, rescued his mother and after greater conflicts he managed to defeat the serpents.

In another episode, the serpent Kaliya stole offerings meant for Garuda, whereupon a fierce battle ensued. Kaliya escaped into the Kalindi pool, only later to be subdued there by Krishna.

But a certain ambiguity is connected with this popular duo. Since they are half brothers, other legends describe the reconciliation between Garuda and the serpents.

Another relationship, which is much more secure, is that of Visnu with Garuda, who serves as the vehicle of the god. In Indian art they are always depicted in symbiotic connection.

Thanks to S.A. Dange and Wendy Doniger.

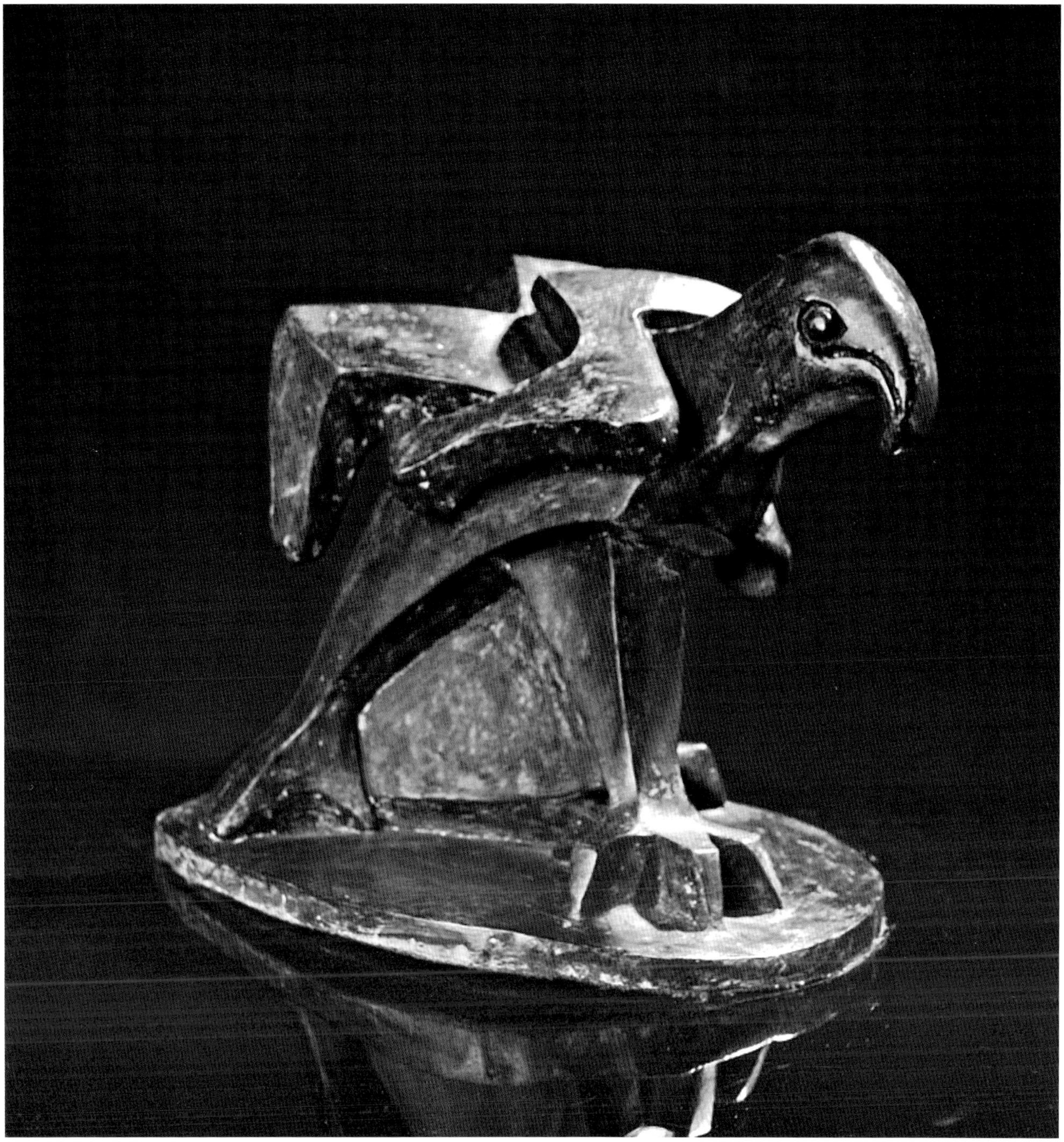

Fig. 47: **Garuda battles serpent (Naga)**

Carmel Berkson,
Bronze, 12" x 9" x 13"

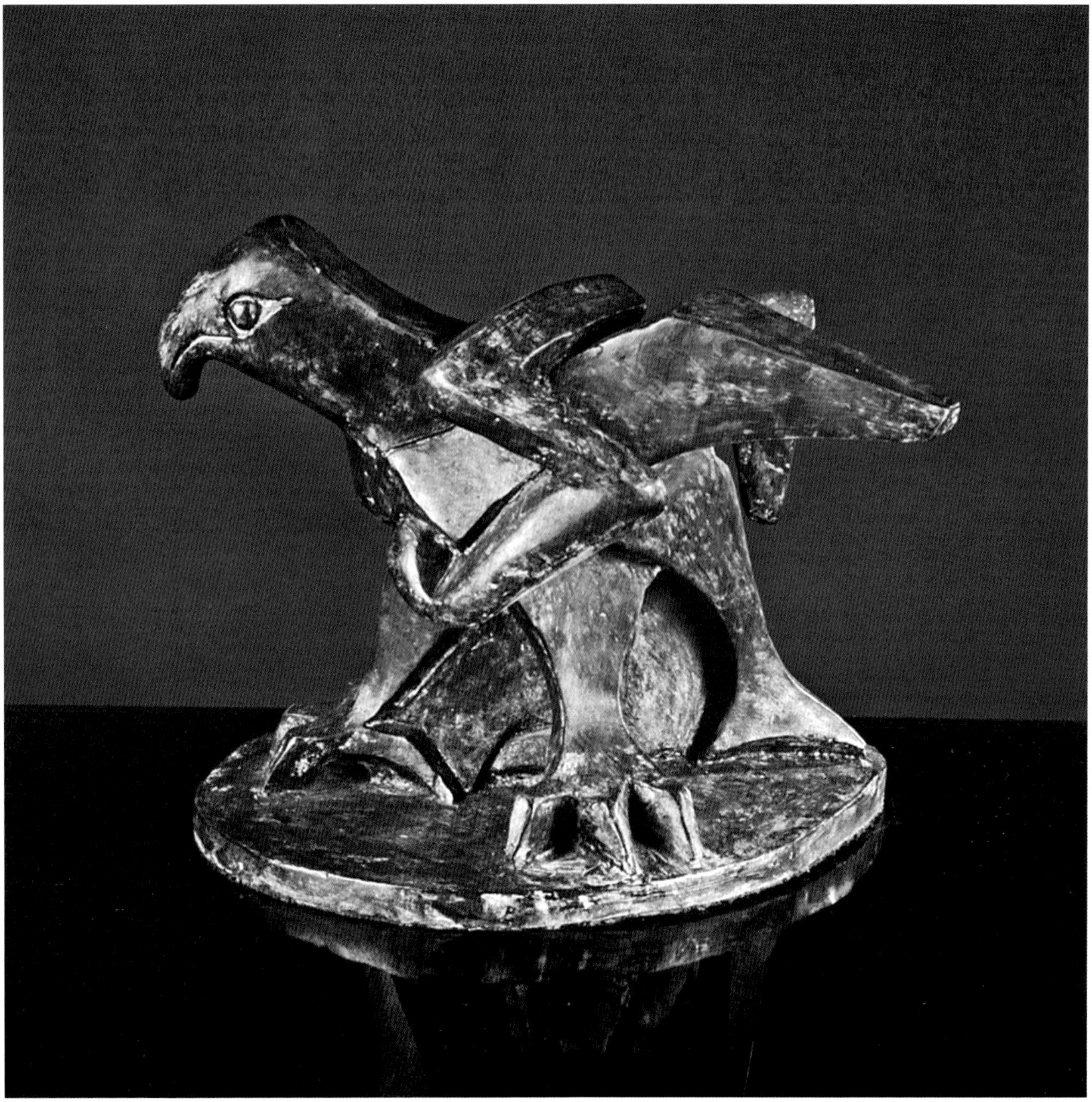

Fig. 48: **Garuda battles serpent (Naga)**

Carmel Berkson,
Bronze, 12" x 9" x 13"

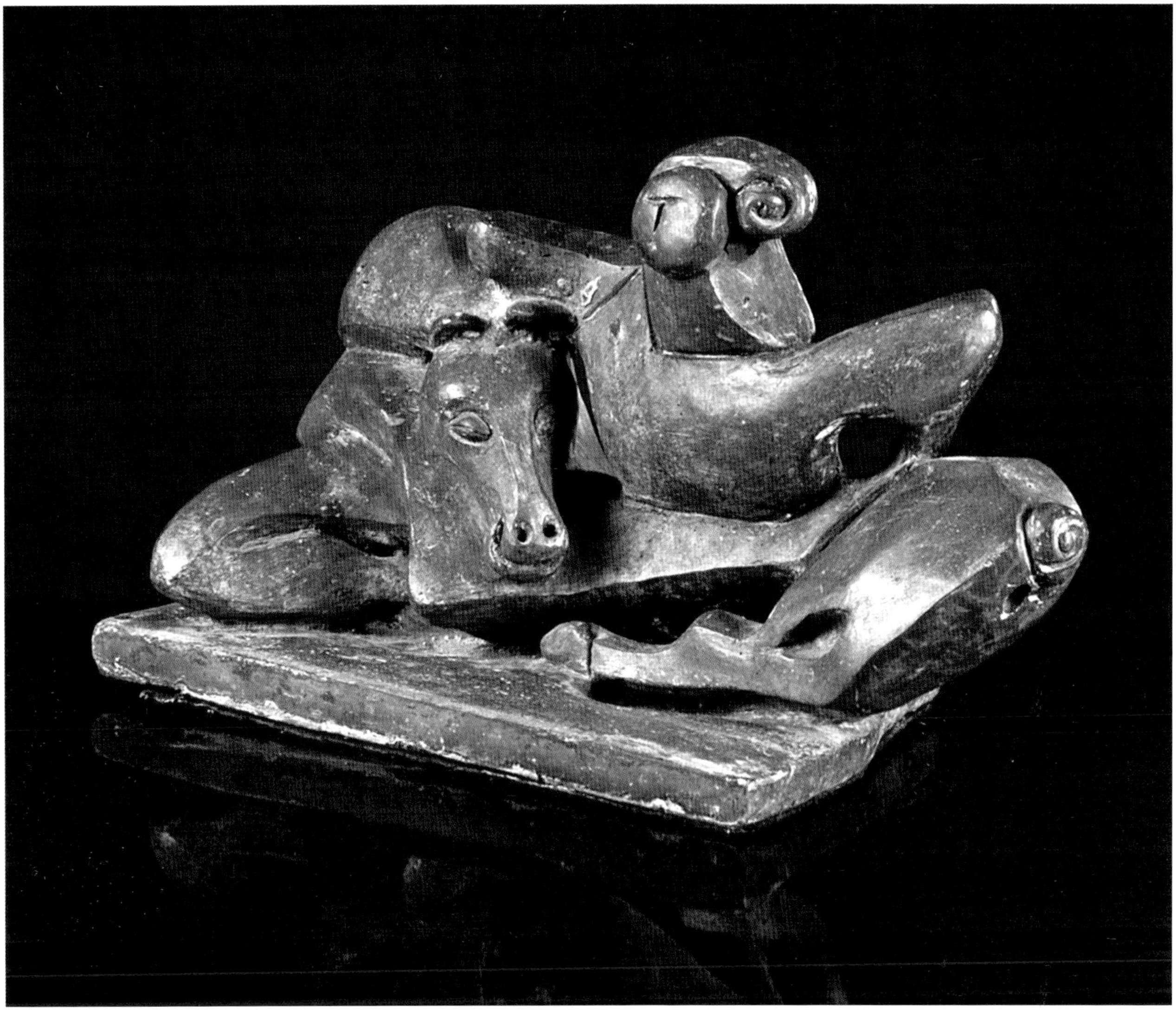

Fig. 49: **Krishna slays Kesava, the horse demon**

Carmel Berkson,
Bronze, 15½" x 10" x 11"

Krishna kills Kesava, the Horse Demon
(Figs. 49-50)

King Kamsa steadfastedly devised many ways to destroy the boy Krishna, who was destined to kill him. He sent the demon Kesin to Vraja in the guise of the horse Kesava. Much to Kamsa's never ending chagrin, Krishna easily defeated the horse in a prolonged battle.

Motifs

1. Child god incarnated in human form
2. Saviour destroys enemies

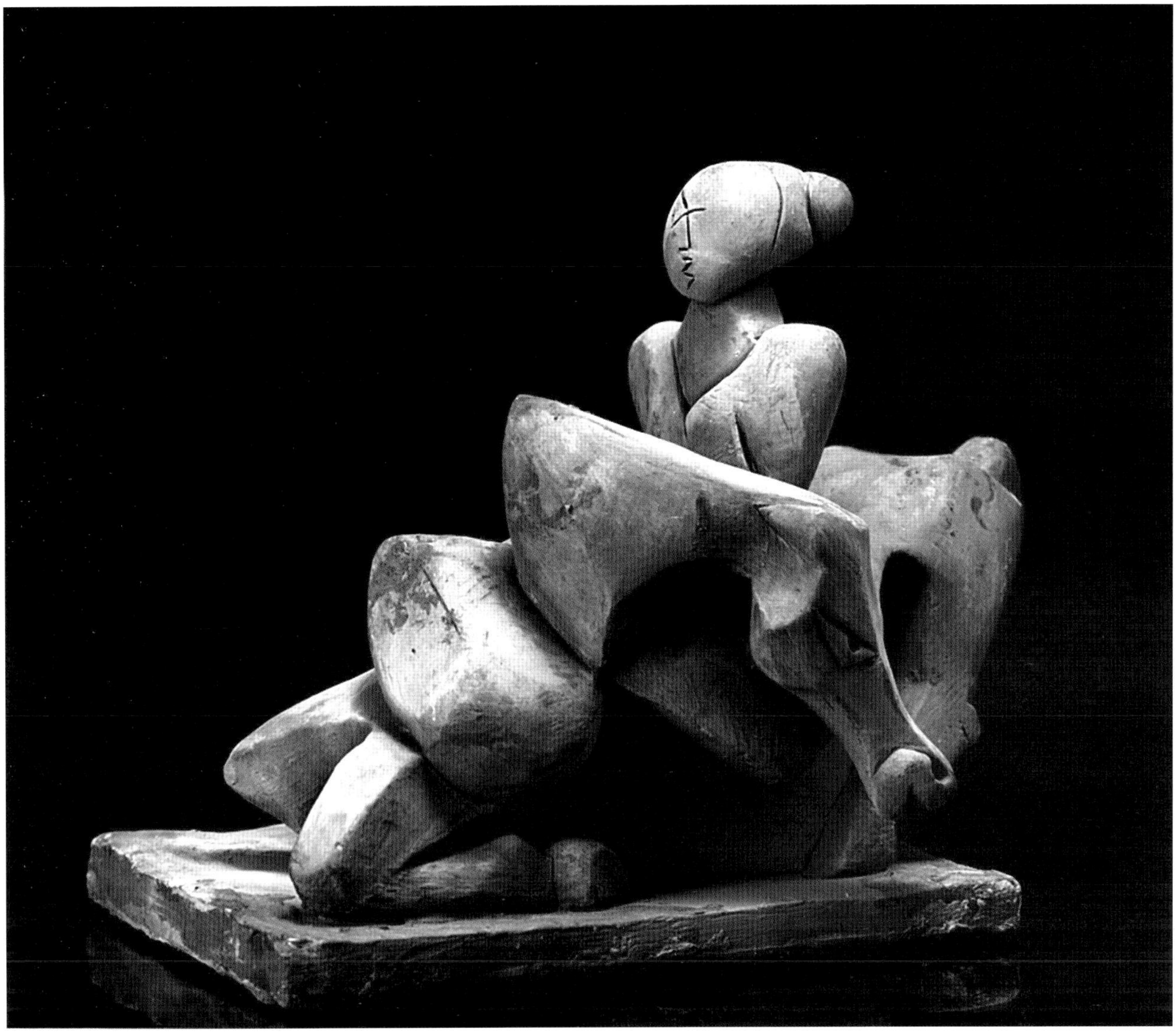

Fig. 50: **Krishna slays Kesava, the horse demon**

Carmel Berkson,
Terracotta, 15½" x 10" x 12"

Krishna and Sachi seek the Parijata Tree (Fig. 51)

The *Parijata* tree was produced during the churning of the ocean.

The bark was gold, and it was embellished with young sprouting leaves of a copper colour and fruit stalks bearing numerous clusters of fragrant fruit. To please his wife, Sachi, Indra planted the tree in heaven. In Dwarka, however, one of Krishna's many wives heard of the *Parijata* tree and sighed and sighed, begging it for herself, so off Krishna and Satyabhama flew to heaven on Garuda to see if they could find a way to possess it. When they reached heaven, Krishna stole into Indra's garden and uprooted the tree. But as he was about to place it on Garuda, he was stopped by Indra's guards, who explained that it actually belonged to Indra's queen Sachi. Satyabhama remonstrated and Sachi appealed to her husband, so there followed a long battle between Indra and Krishna, each intent on acquiring the tree for his own wife.

Finally, because of his great respect for Krishna, Indra relented and urged him to take the tree. Back on Garuda, Krishna and Satyabhama flew to their home in Dwarka. The Visnu Purana ends the story: "Then, alighting from Garuda, Krishna proceeded with Satyabhama to her garden and there planted the great *Parijata* tree, the smell of which perfumes the earth and an approach to which enables everyone to recollect the events of a prior existence."[1]

The statue depicts Krishna and Satyabhama on Garuda in their flight up to heaven.

Motifs

1. Gods share human frailties
2. Gods are powerful but not liberated
3. Greed, envy shared by humans and gods
4. Sacred tree

---

[1]Visnu Purana, Chapter 30.

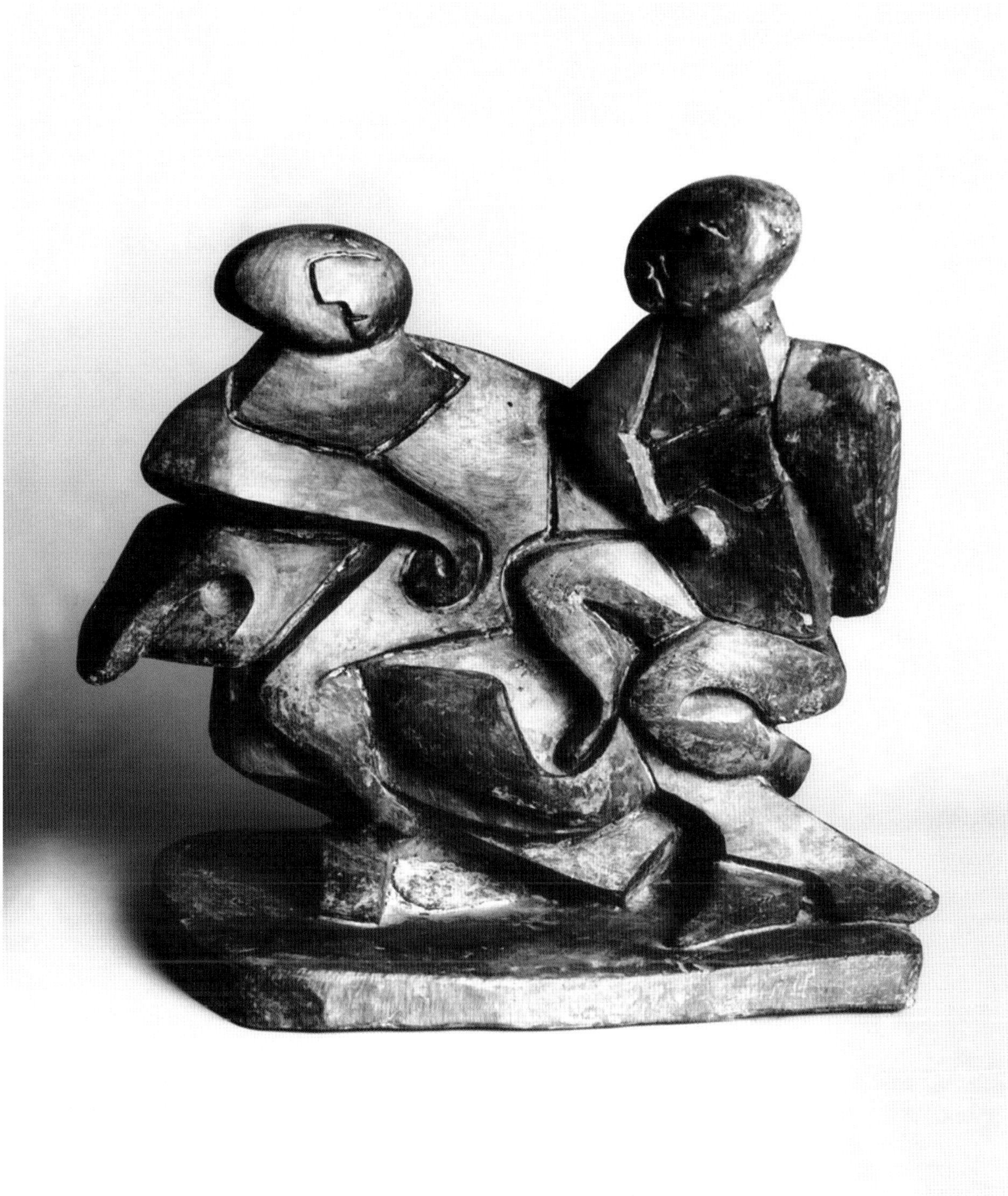

Fig. 51: **Krishna and Sachi seek the Parijata Tree**

Carmel Berkson,
Bronze, 12" x 9" x 14"

Krishna subdues Kaliya
(Figs. 52-53)

Krishna's cows and cowherds drank from the boiling Kalindi pool within the Jamuna river, but all became ill from the poison emitted from the mouth of the giant, many-hooded cobra, Kaliya. After reviving them with his breath, in order to protect the waters for the people, Krishna plunged into a ferocious battle with Kaliya. At first, it appeared as though the struggle would end disastrously for Krishna, as he was caught in the coils of the serpent, who spewed poison, but Krishna's marvellous powers soon subdued the terrible serpent demon. He expanded and then extracted himself from the coils and danced on the head of Kaliya. Krishna did not kill Kaliya, but out of compassion for its wives, he banished it to a far ocean.

Motifs

1. Child god incarnated in human form
2. Saviour destroys enemies
3. Compassionate god forgives enemy

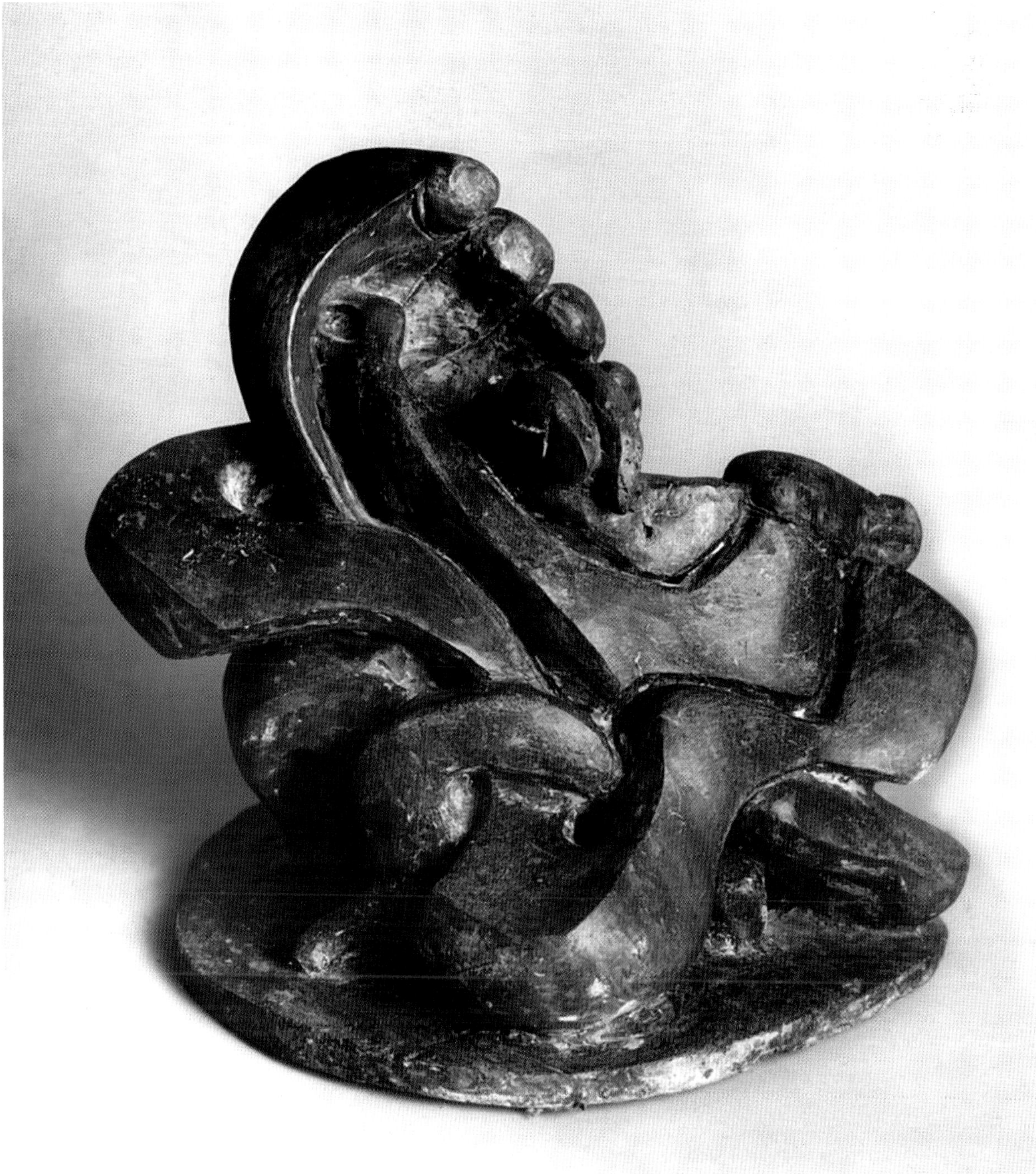

Fig. 52: **Krishna subdues Kaliya**

Carmel Berkson,
Bronze, 13" x 10" x 14"

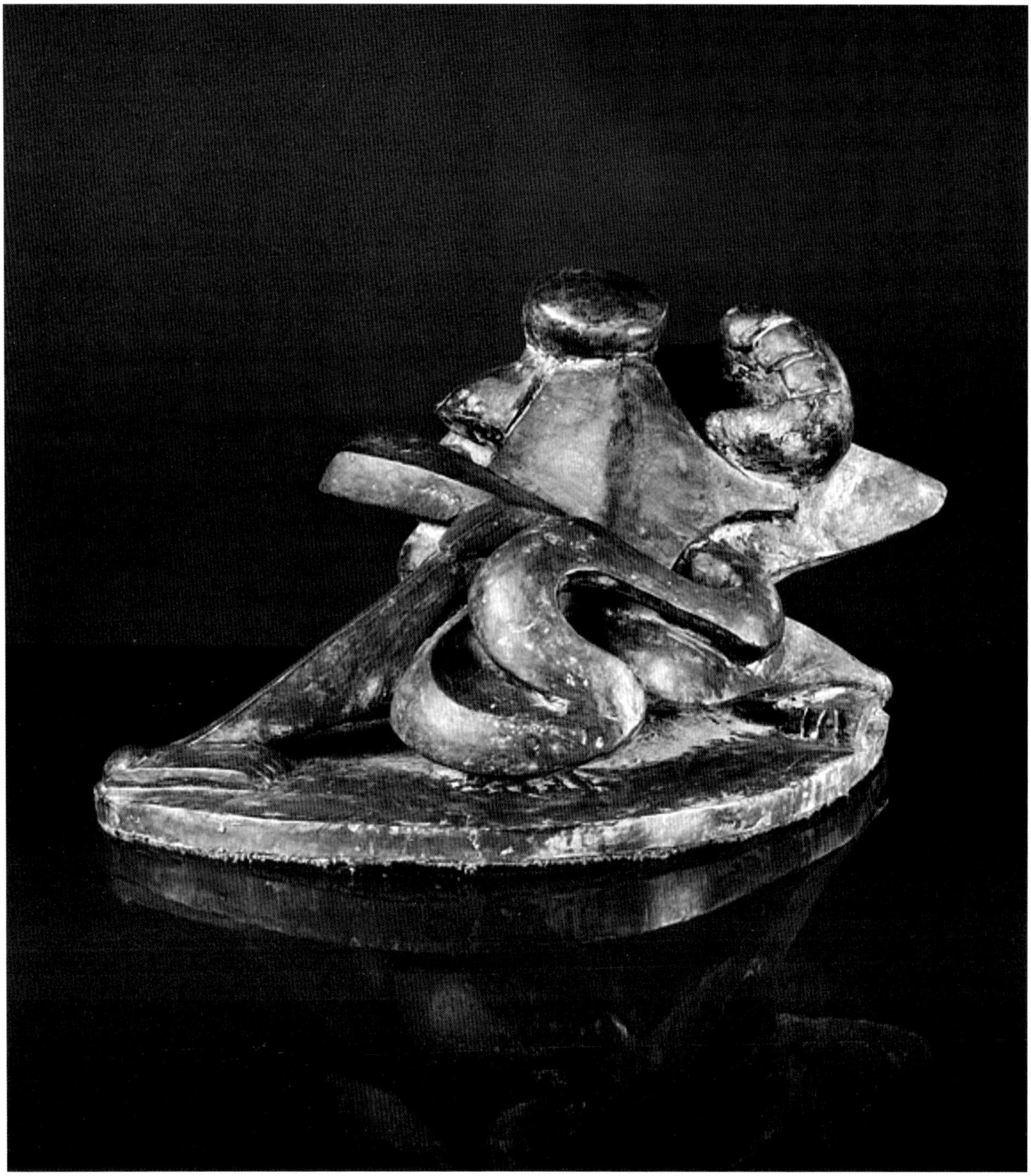

Fig. 53: **Krishna subdues Kaliya**

Carmel Berkson,
Bronze, 15" x 9" x 9"

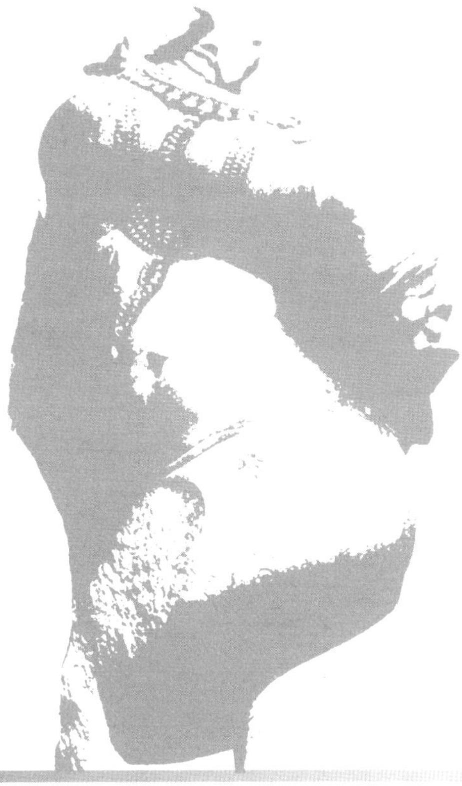

Rasa

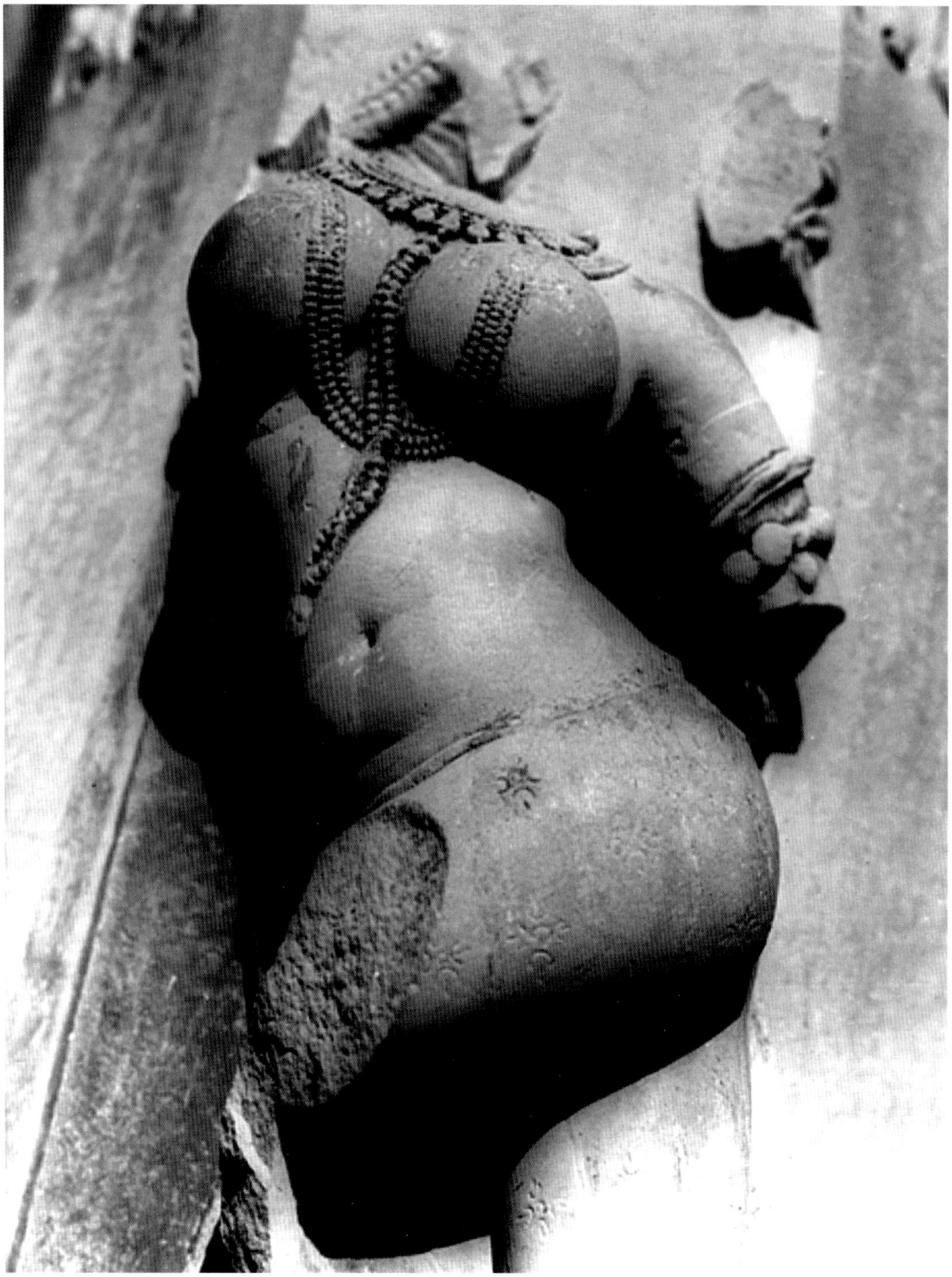

Fig. 54: **Rasa: *Shringara* (erotic love)**

Apsara on Column, Siva Temple, Badoli, Rajasthan, 11th c. C.E.

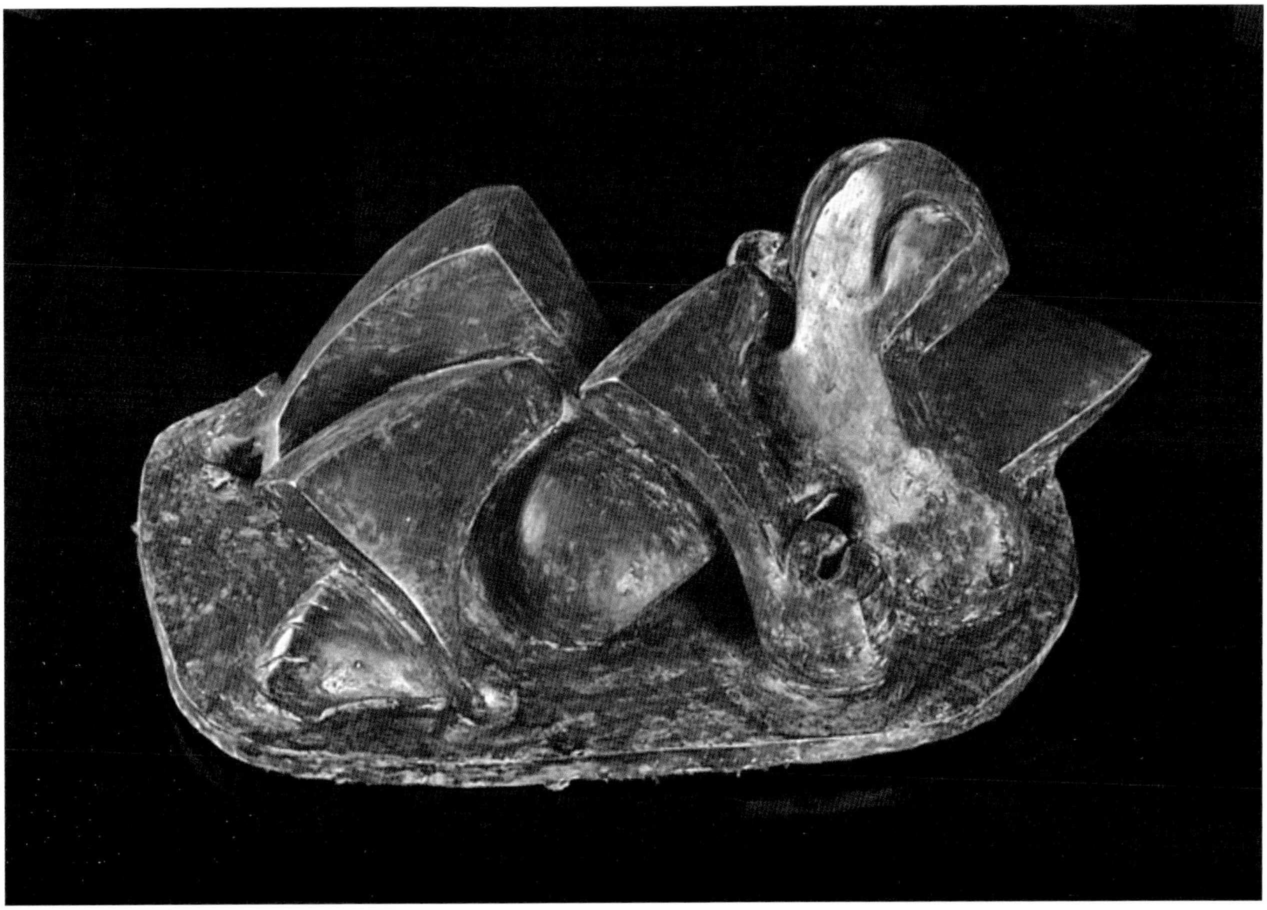

Fig. 55: **Rasa: *Shringara* (erotic love)**

Reclining Nude
Carmel Berkson,
Bronze, 14" x 10" x 7½"

Ruth and Boaz
(Fig. 56)

During a famine, a man and his wife went from Bethlehem in Judea with their two sons to Moab. There the sons married Moabite women, but the father and sons did not survive. The mother, Naomi, returned to Bethlehem with her daughter-in-law, the Moabite Ruth.

Boaz, a near relative, was a wealthy farmer; in compassion for the two poor women he permitted Ruth to glean the remainder of the barley crop on his farm during harvest time. Since he was being so concerned, at the advice of Naomi, Ruth came silently to stay at the feet of Boaz as he slept one night in his field. Soon thereafter, Boaz married Ruth. Their child Obed was the grandfather of David.

Old Testament: Book of Ruth.

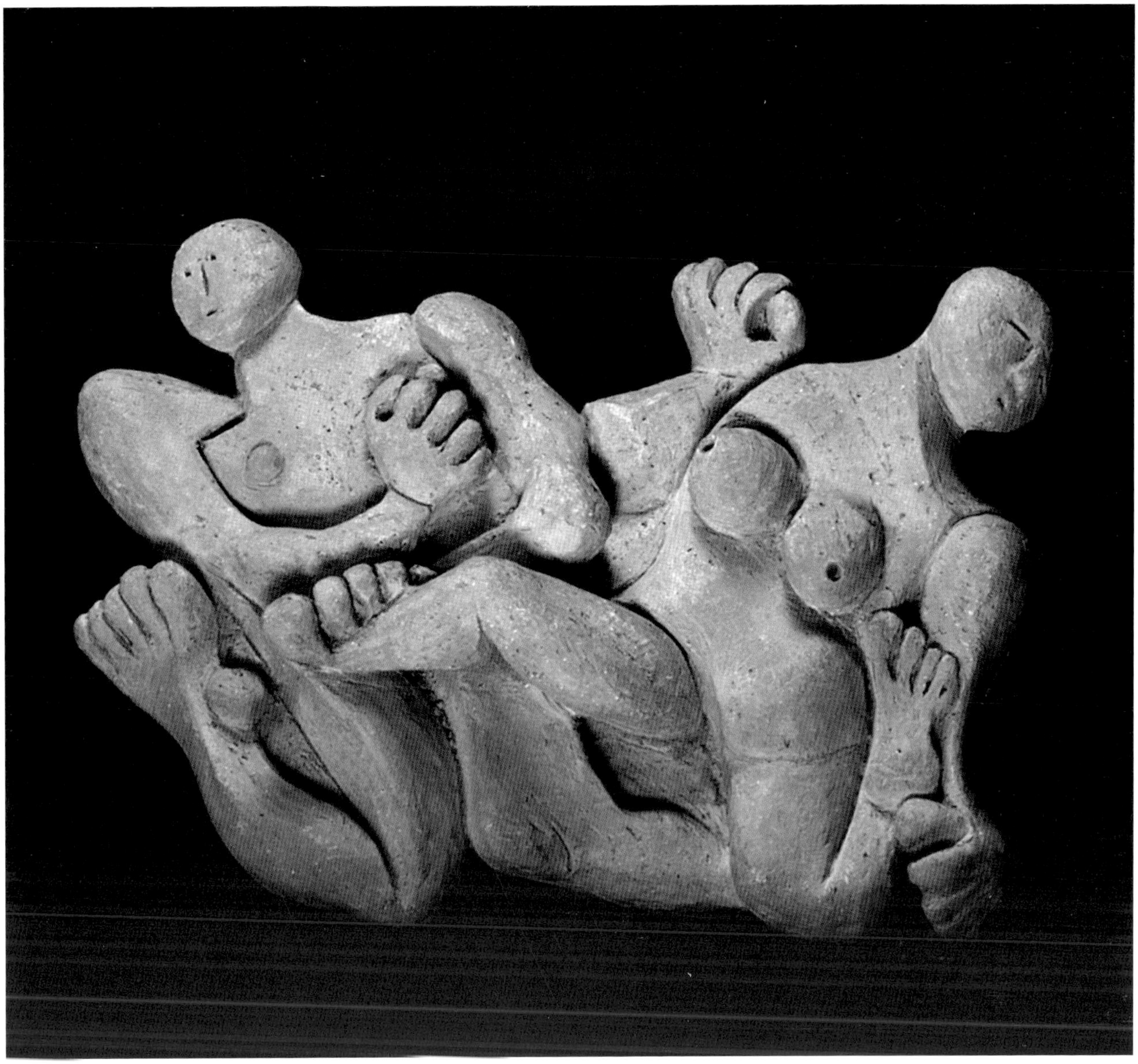

Fig. 56: **Rasa: *Shringara* (erotic love)**

Ruth and Boaz
Carmel Berkson,
Bronze, bas relief: 10" x 9"

Yab-Yum
(Figs. 57-59)

The composition is inspired by the Tantric/Esoteric Buddhist imagery of male and female deities in ritual sexual embrace. By associating his or her own experiences with those of the union of the gods, the votary achieves an intimation of the bliss and ecstasy of non-duality and enlightenment, which is the ultimate goal of the rites of release from temporal bonds.

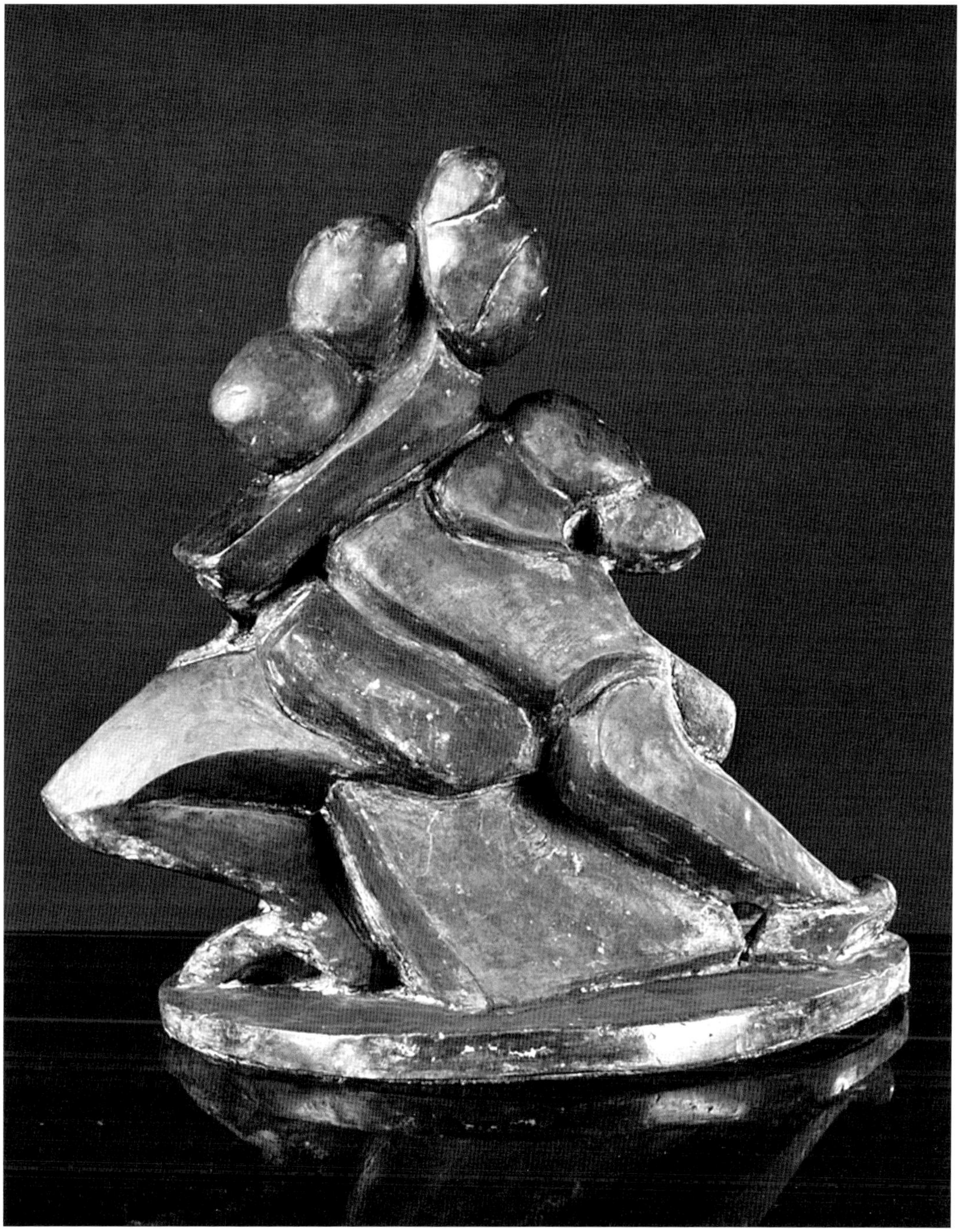

Fig. 57: **Rasa: *Shringara* (erotic love)**

Yab-Yum
Carmel Berkson,
Bronze, 13" x 10" x 15"

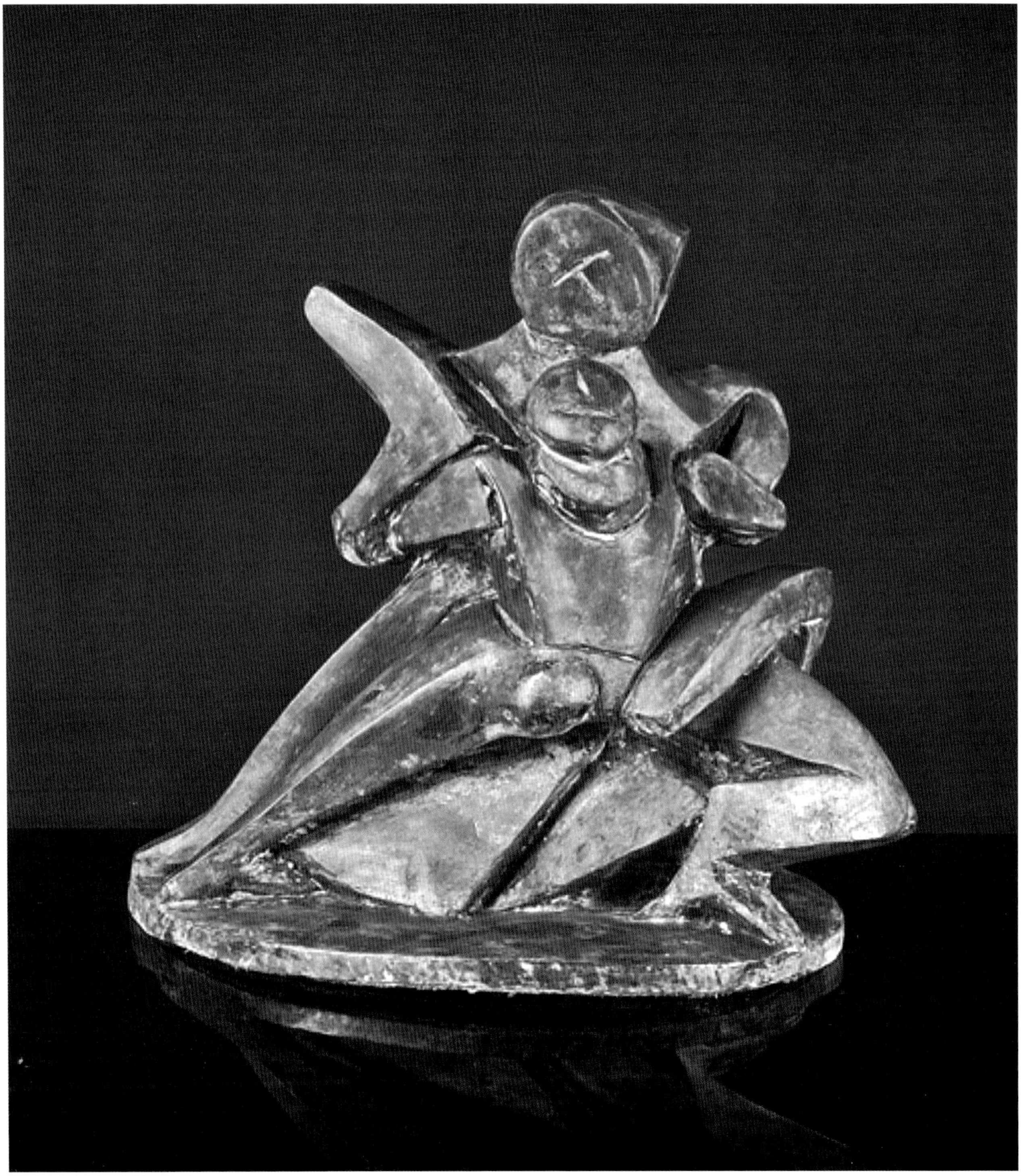

Fig. 58: **Rasa: *Shringara* (erotic love)**

Yab-Yum
Carmel Berkson,
Bronze, 13" x 10" x 15"

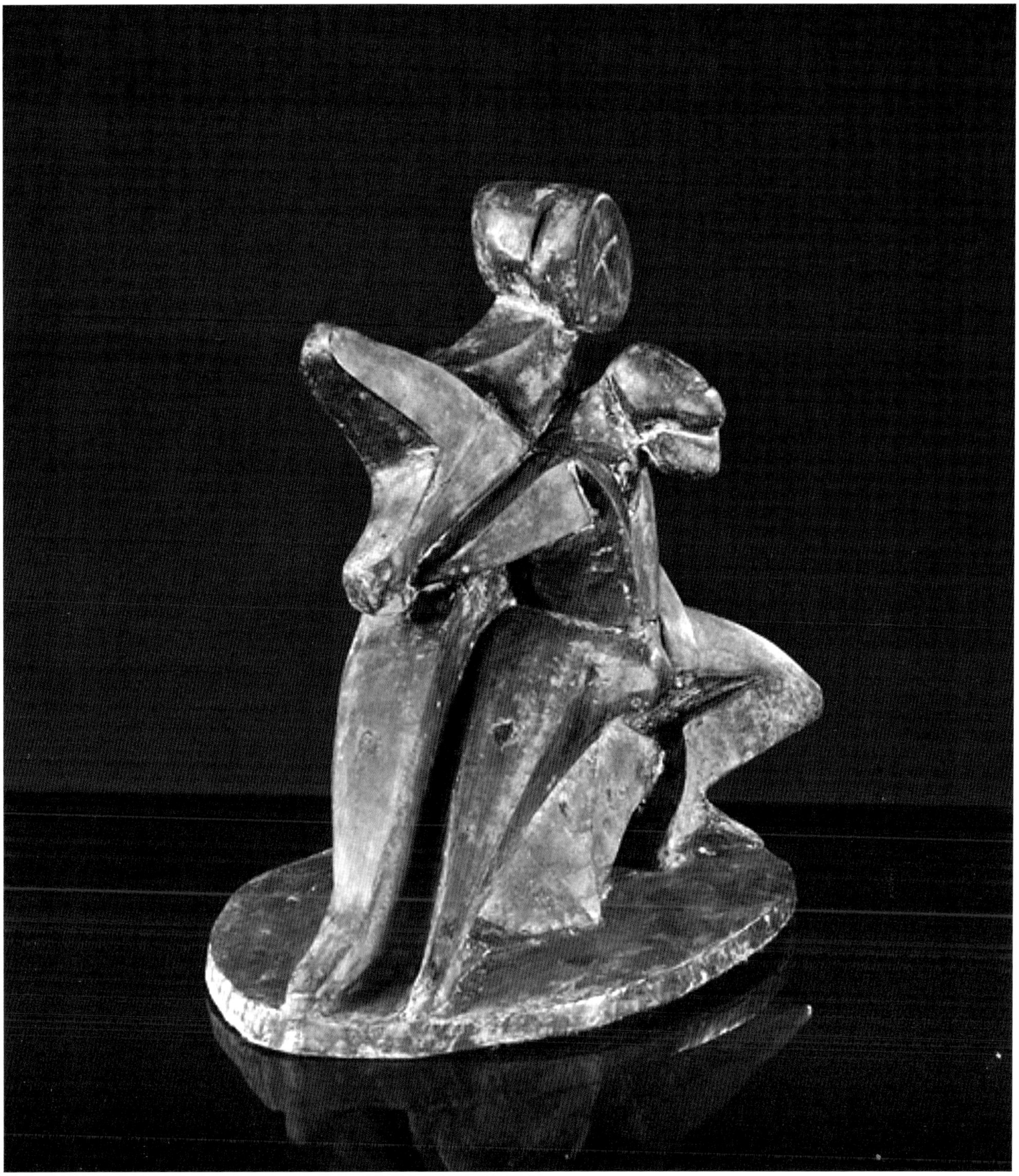

Fig. 59: **Rasa: *Shringara* (erotic love)**

Yab-Yum
Carmel Berkson,
Bronze, 13" x 10" x 15"

Amazon
(Fig. 60)

This composition was inspired by a Greek sarcophagus which depicted the Amazon on her horse in battle with Theseus. In Greek mythology and art, the one-breasted female warriors live in isolated communities and are trained in the use of all weaponry, in hand to hand and single battle techniques. The concept of this beautiful feminine image spread throughout the world, signifying male/female oppositions. At Mamallapuram in Tamil Nadu, the great panel depicting the goddess in battle with Mahisha has many stylistic relationships to the Amazon sarcophagus in the Rockefeller Museum, Jerusalem.

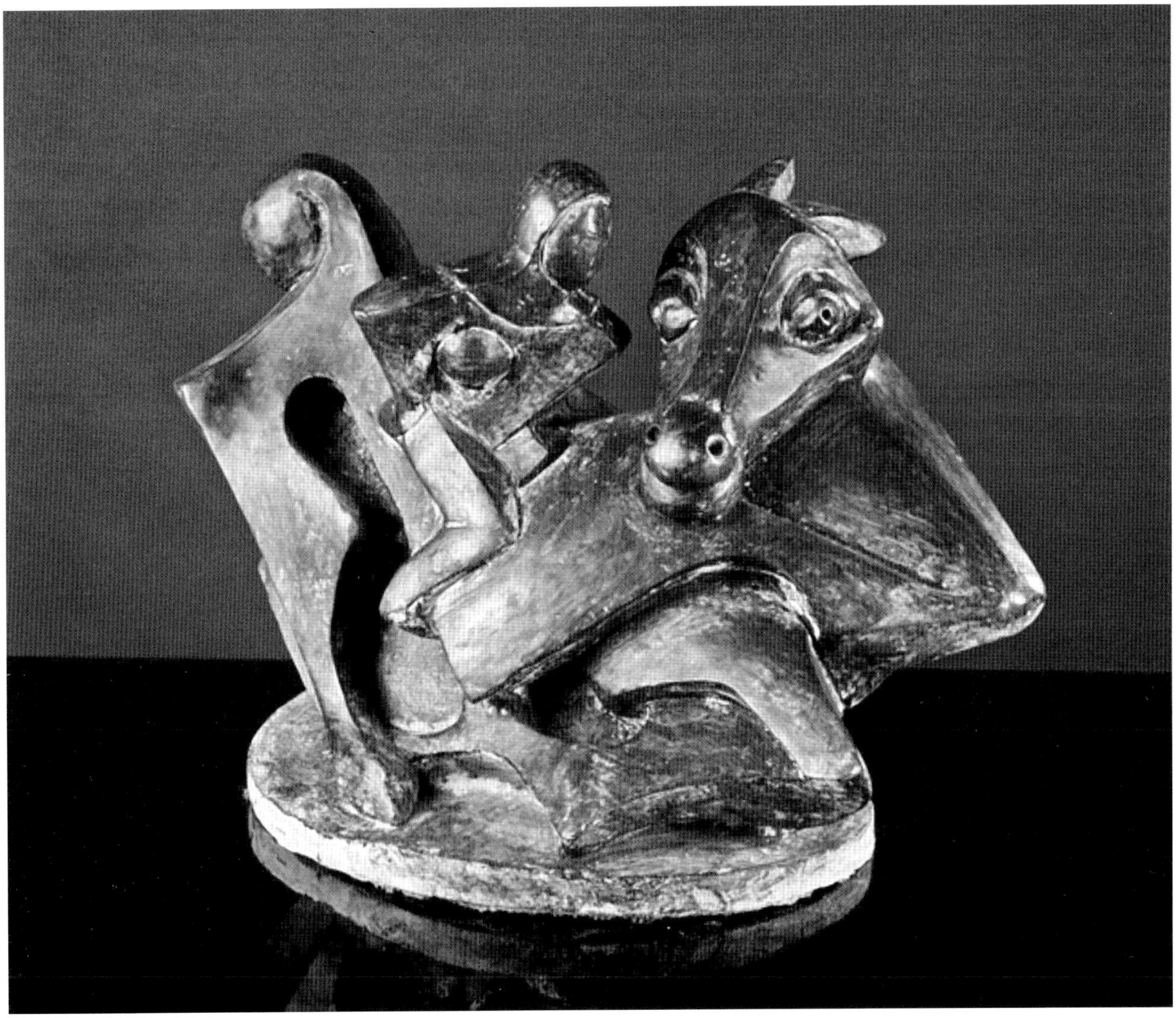

Fig. 60: **Rasa: *Raudra* (furious, anger)**

Amazon
Carmel Berkson,
Bronze, 14" x 10" x 12"

David and Absalom (Fig. 61)

There had always been tension between King David and one of his many sons – Absalom. Albeit for a good reason: Absalom had murdered Amnon, his half brother. King David thereupon banished Absalom from Jerusalem, but within three years, he was permitted to return.

Absalom proceeded to conspire against his father and with much guile managed to gain many loyal Israelite warriors. A long period of enmity divided Israel from Judah, and father from son, although David persistently ordered his men: "Deal gently, for my sake, with the young man; beware lest anyone touch the young man, Absalom."

Ultimately Absalom's forces were vanquished. As he rode on a mule: "The mule went under the thick boughs of a great terebinth tree, and his head caught in the terebinth; so he was left hanging between heaven and earth. Soon thereafter, unbeknownst to King David, his officer speared to death the living Absalom and buried him thereafter."

This statue is my image of paternal feelings as expressed in David's lament when he heard the news.

> "Oh, Absalom, my son, my son,
> Would to god I had died for thee, my son."

Motifs

1. Fratricide
2. Oedipal antagonisms
3. Paternal ambiguity concerning son

Old Testament: II Samuel, Chap. 18.

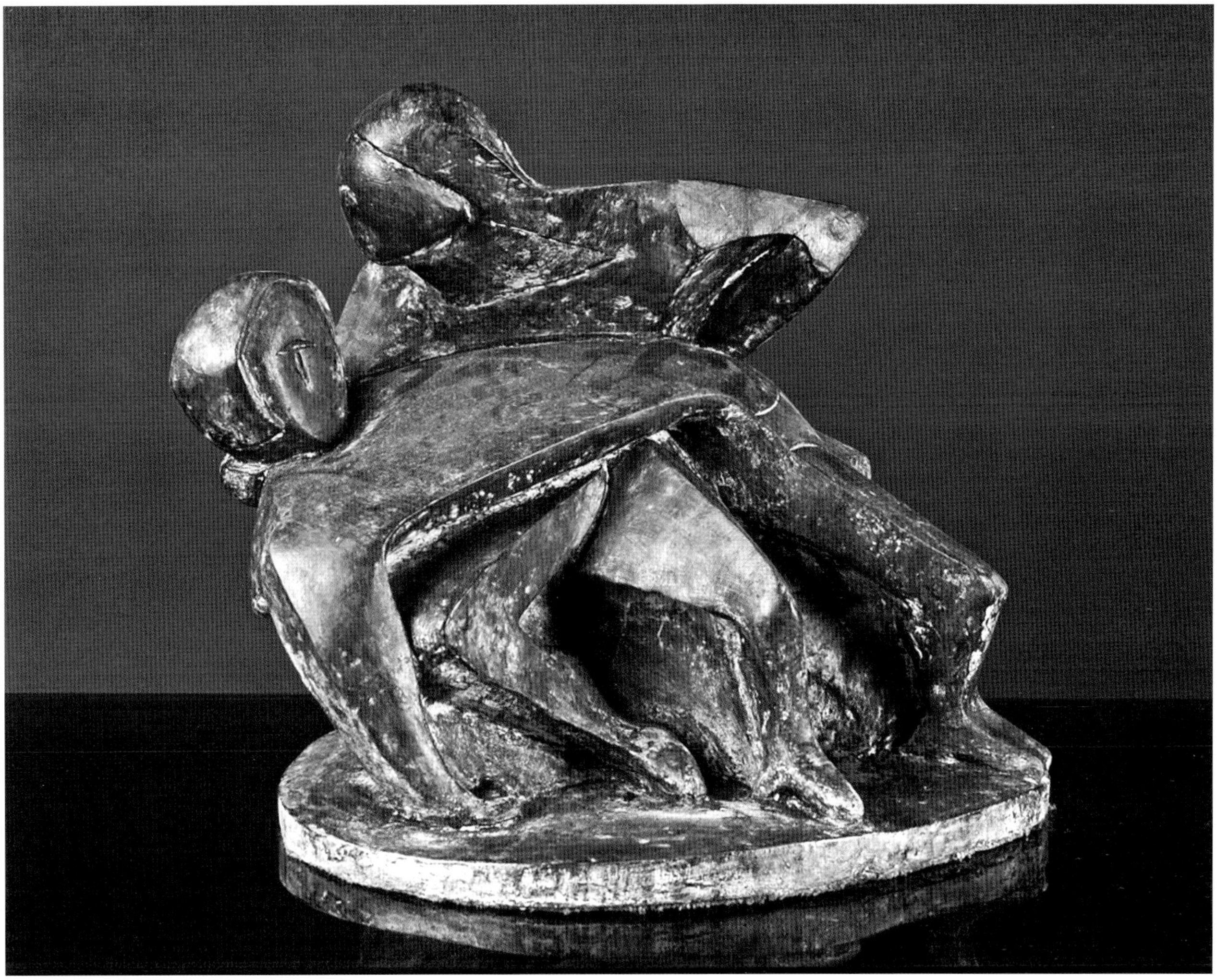

Fig. 61: **Rasa: *Karuna* (sorrow, compassion)**

David and Absalom
Carmel Berkson,
Bronze, 12" x 9" x 9"

Bodhisattva and Dying Warrior
(Figs. 62, 63)

There doesn't seem to be a solution to universal wars and perpetual death of youth. It would therefore seem that the only possible human response is, at the very least, for the human psyche to maintain connection with the tendency to feel compassion, as symbolized by the Buddhist *bodhisattva*.

Motifs

1. Compassion
2. Death of youth

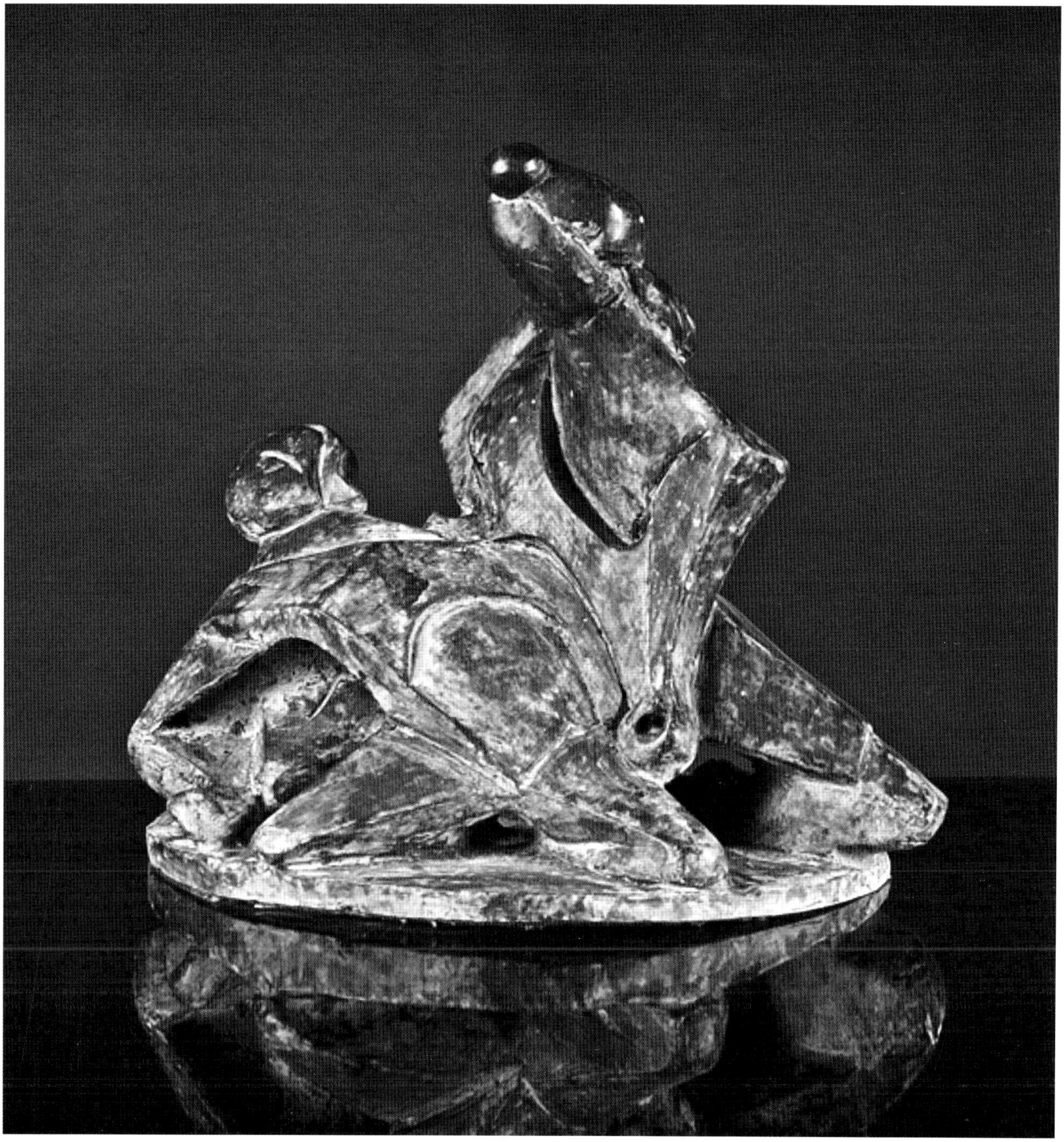

Fig. 62: **Rasa: *Karuna* (sorrow, compassion)**

Bodhisattva and dying warrior
Carmel Berkson,
Bronze, 15" x 11" x 14"

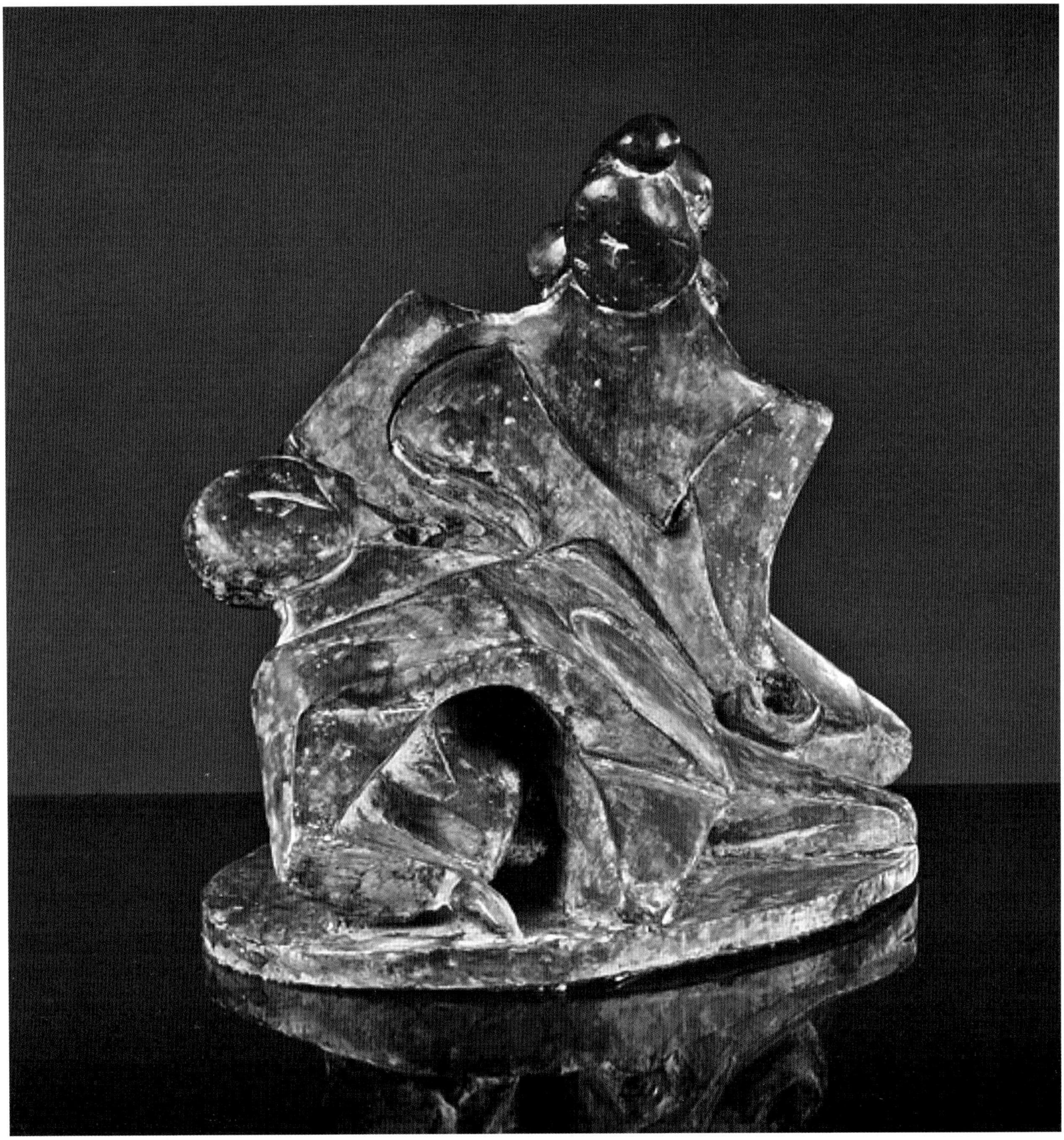

Fig. 63: **Rasa: *Karuna* (sorrow, compassion)**

Bodhisattva and dying warrior
Carmel Berkson,
Bronze, 15" x 11" x 14"

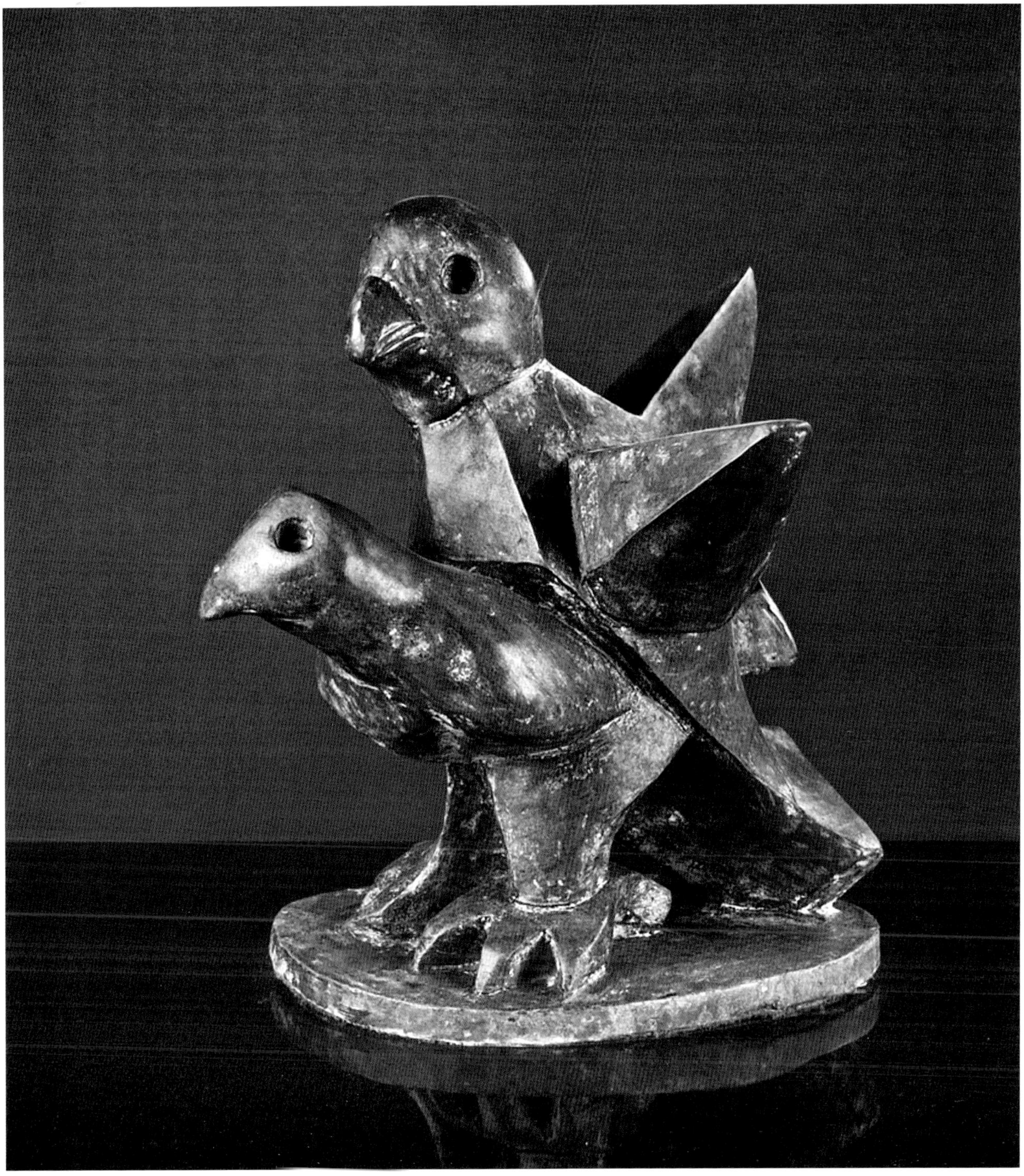

Fig. 64: **Rasa:** ***Karuna*** **(compassion)**

Two birds
Carmel Berkson,
Bronze, 11" x 7" x 14"

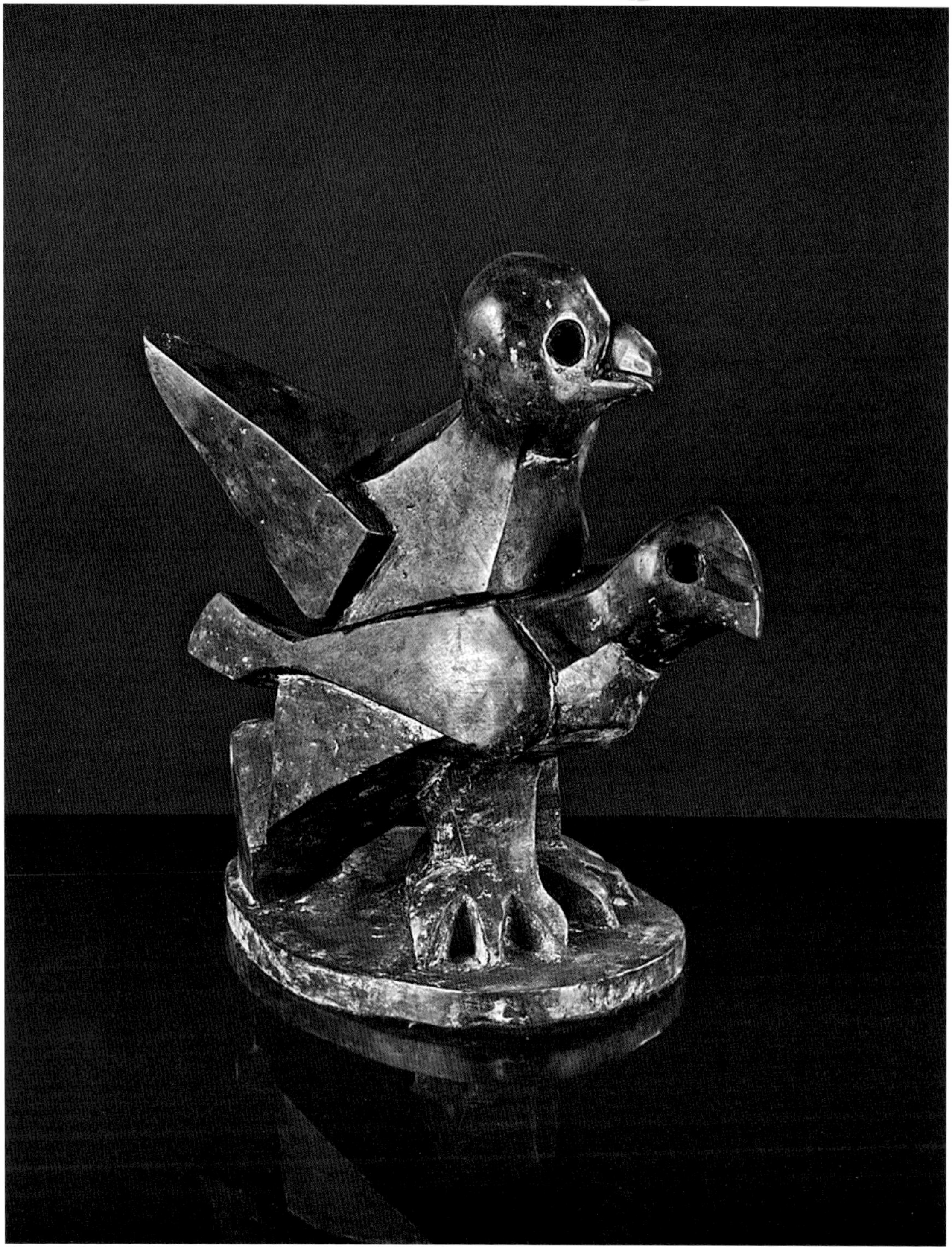

Fig. 65: **Rasa: *Karuna* (compassion)**

Two birds
Carmel Berkson,
Bronze, 11" x 7" x 14"

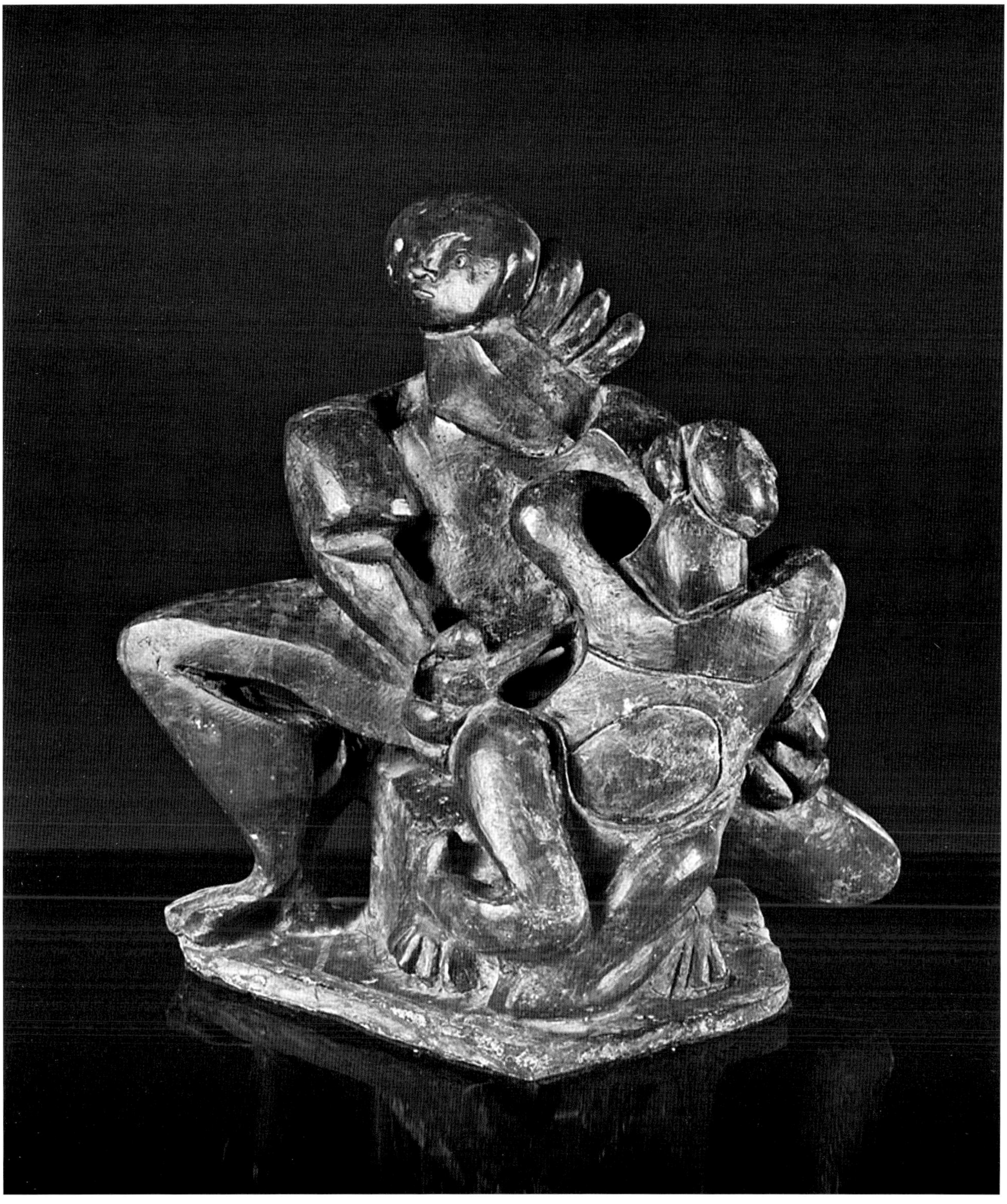

Fig. 66: **Rasa: *Bhayanaka* (terrible, fear)**

The sacrifice of the first-born
Carmel Berkson,
Bronze, 10½" x 9" x 13½"

The Sacrifice of the First-Born

(Figs. 66, 67, 68)

The sacrifice of the first-born son in order to propitiate totem or deity was universally practised from primordial onward into historical times. In many cultures, the memory is retained in symbolic motifs, in rituals and in works of art which function as an attempt at amelioration or sublimation of a human force buried deeply even in the contemporary psyche.

The statue is a paradigm, an agglomerate of varying versions. The Bible records the intended sacrifice of Isaac by Abraham. In the Hindu scriptures, we read about Paruncoti who killed his son, cooked him and served Siva with the meal and of Agastha who sold his son Sunasepha as a substitute for Rohita, whose father had promised Varuna a sacrificial gift of a son. And there were more, many more. The prime motif is the same, a father, wishing to propitiate a god, will either commit the murder of his son or have the intent to do so but is stopped at the last moment. Often there are contradicting ambiguities to counter the terrifying internal force.

Motif

Filicide

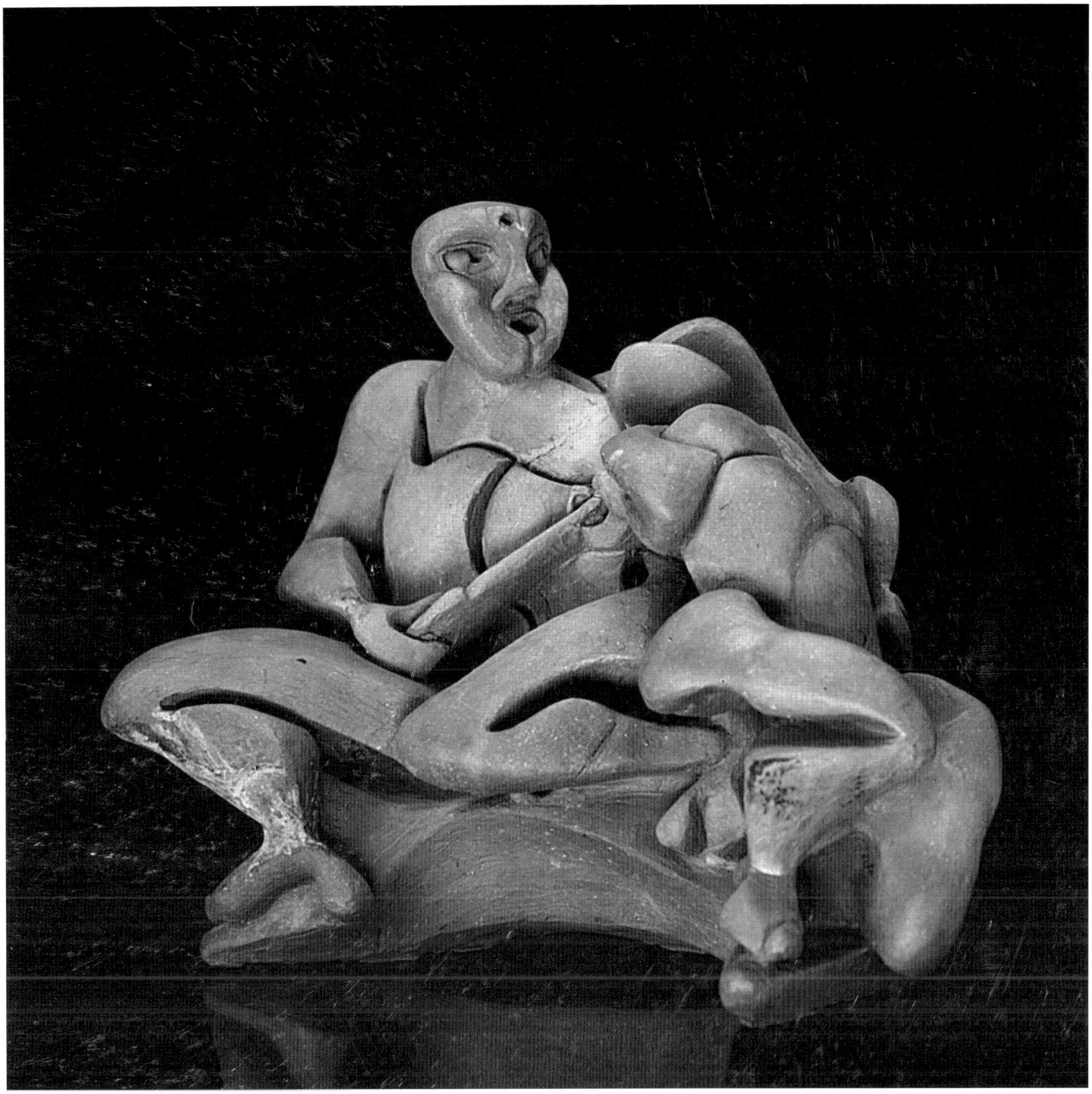

Fig. 67: **Rasa: *Bhayanaka* (terrible, fear)**

The sacrifice of the first-born
Carmel Berkson,
Bronze, 9" x 7" x 13"

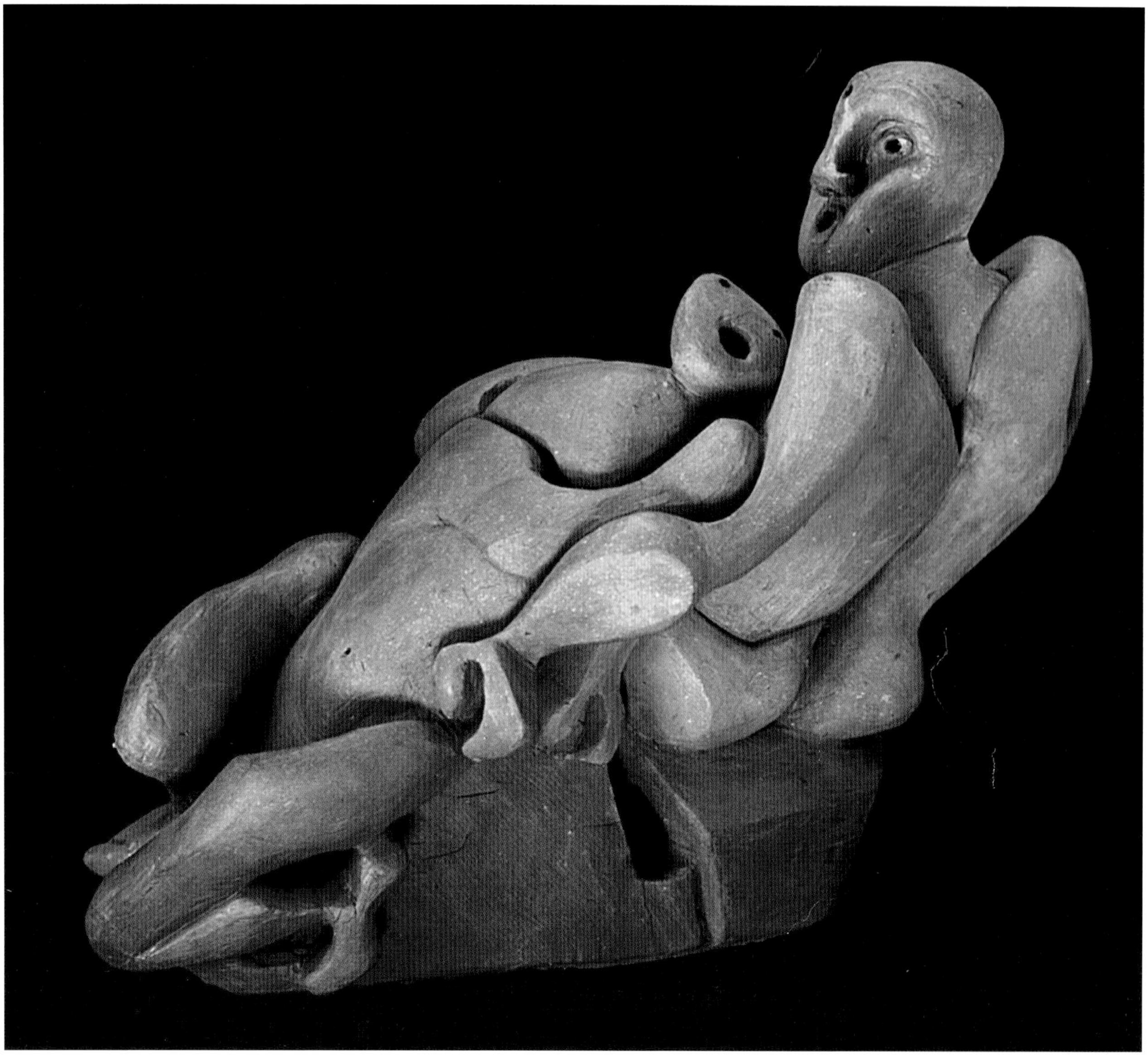

Fig. 68: **Rasa: *Bhayanaka* (terrible, fear)**

The sacrifice of the first-born
Carmel Berkson,
Bronze, 9" x 7" x 13"